Keeping a Free Republic: Learning the Blueprint for Liberty in the Constitution & the Bill of Rights

by

Paul Dowling

Inspired Quotes

"Well, Doctor," Mrs. Powel queried, "what have we got, a republic or a monarchy?" "A republic, madam," Dr. Franklin replied, "if you can keep it." —A famous exchange between an American woman and Dr. Benjamin Franklin, warning of the vigilance required for keeping a republic

"The Citizens of the United States of America have a right to applaud themselves for giving to Mankind examples of an enlarged and liberal policy: a policy worthy of imitation. All possess alike liberty of conscience and immunities of citizenship. It is now no more that toleration is spoken of, as if it was by the indulgence of one class of people that another enjoyed the exercise of their inherent natural rights. For happily the Government of the United States, which gives to bigotry no sanction, to persecution no assistance, requires only that they who live under its protection, should demean themselves as good citizens." —George Washington, from an August 18th, 1790, letter to the Congregation Kahal Kadosh Yeshuat Israel (now known as the Touro Synagogue) of Newport Rhode Island, wherein he refers to republican toleration and protection of the rights of all individuals and minorities

"In questions of powers, then, let no more be heard of confidence in man, but bind him down from mischief by the chains of the Constitution." —Thomas Jefferson, urging that the Constitution be trusted above politicians and that it be constantly invoked

Copyright Page

Copyright © 2018 by Paul Dennis Dowling
All Contents © Paul Dennis Dowling

About The Author

Paul Dowling grew up in Baytown, Texas, where he learned to value family, friends, and freedom. He earned a B.A. in Linguistics and an M.A. in German from the University of Texas at Austin, continuing his studies at the University of Houston, where he went on to earn an M.A. in English and an Ed.D. in Curriculum & Instruction.

A public school teacher of three decades' experience, in both Texas and California, Paul currently lives in Texas, where he enables freedom by working as a life-skills coach and career counselor who helps special education students procure job preparation and competitive employment, as well as postsecondary education and work training.

Paul has volunteered as a docent at the Ronald Reagan Presidential Library and Museum in Simi Valley, California, and has sponsored a high school Constitution Club. He enjoys studying American history, the US Constitution, the Hebrew Bible, and economic theory, as well as writing articles for *Eagle Rising* (https://eaglerising.com/author/paul-dowling/). Paul also enjoys giving speeches to educate others about correct principles for the maintenance of a free republic.

Contents

Dedication

To Carole, a God-fearing American patriot who believes that America is a shining city on a hill and who encourages me to fight for freedom, in parlance and in print, to enlighten and inspire all lovers of liberty who wish to hear the truth about America and its blessings. Thank you, Carole.

Acknowledgments

I wish first to acknowledge my relationship with God, Whose holy word inspires me daily and Whose gift of two wonderful parents has proven to be an ongoing blessing in my life. The knowledge that any accomplishments of mine all depend on God-given talents means that I must do honor to the gifts God has given me. Also, I must strive to be a blessing to the world by helping others to recognize and to share their blessings as well.

My parents, Patsy and Dennis, have blessed my life tremendously. My mother, of blessed memory, was my number one cheerleader and a fan of every enterprise I undertook. My father offered me—and continues to offer—valuable insights and constructive criticisms, while encouraging me to step forward with any knowledge or talent that might prove valuable in helping to improve and repair the world.

My daughter Na Yeon has always encouraged my writing and has always believed passionately in what I have to say. I am thankful for her critical, yet sensitive and appreciative, eye at times when I have needed exactly that.

I should also like to recognize Onan Coca for his encouraging me to write for the online periodical where he is editor, *Eagle Rising* (which can be found at http://eaglerising.com/). Onan has demonstrated a commitment to publishing many different viewpoints from within the big tent of Constitutional conservatism. Working to create meaningful articles for the audience of *Eagle Rising* has only helped me in my efforts to become a more sensitive writer. Thank you, Onan, for blessing me with a platform from which I might speak out. God bless you!

Author's Preface: Tipping the Scale for Liberty

"Then Abraham approached Him and said: 'Will you sweep away the righteous along with the wicked? What if there be fifty righteous people in the city? Would you really sweep it away and not spare the place for the sake of the fifty righteous people in it?'" —Abraham, asking that God act to protect the minority, in Genesis 18:23-24

I had a dream.

A man with his back to me was speaking to the Author of Creation, with humility balanced against chutzpah, saying, "I know that I am only Your creature, made from the dust of the earth, but it would be a grave injustice for You to doom the righteous people of our free republic along with the wicked! I am grateful to You and am doing my part, according to Your Word, to teach the people to love their neighbors as they love themselves."

And the Divine Presence replied, "The work you are doing is ethical and good. It is in your power to be the last straw—the one that tips the scale. Continue in your struggles and be a blessing to your countrymen."

The man bowed low, then straightened and turned as the Heavenly Vision faded. It was at this point that I saw the man's face. And it looked just like mine.

The dream was an inspiration to me, reinforcing my belief that every individual effort to help Americans learn more about freedom is both of moral and of scale-tipping consequence. Teaching the ethical system of the Founders, based upon the Golden Rule and the safeguards of freedom they framed in the US Constitution, is a worthwhile pursuit; no blueprint for liberty is better for Americans to learn than that of the Constitution. Being religious, I believe God wants us to be free.

Reasonable people, religious or not, are likely to agree that the best life is lived in harmony with the Golden Rule: Love your neighbor as yourself (from *Leviticus 19:18*). Happily, the US Constitution is the Golden Rule *writ large*. Under the Constitution, all people enjoy reciprocity in the living out of Natural Rights and Equal Protection under the law. The Golden Rule also concerns the rule of law and the delivery of justice to one's neighbor as one might expect justice to be done to oneself, per *Deuteronomy 16:20*: "Justice, and only justice, shall you pursue." Hillel, the Jewish sage, frames the Golden Rule thus: "Do not do unto others that which you hate done unto yourself." In other words, "Do not make others into victims, if you yourself would hate being a victim," or "Do not infringe the rights of others, if you jealously guard your own."

The Constitution embeds the Golden Rule throughout its text, guaranteeing that freedom and justice are applied equally under the law for every individual—which means that no American is above the law, not even the president or any other member of the government.

Restoration of the Constitution, as close as possible to its original limits, needs to occur, so that Americans might fully realize their common birthright of liberty. This can never happen, however, unless Americans are correctly educated about Constitutionally-restrained government and the principles that inform it. These principles must be actively appreciated and pursued if freedom is to ring loudly throughout our land.

My hope is that readers will appreciate, as well as share with others, any ideas of value they may learn from reading this book on the "golden rules" that are embedded within our Constitution; for, more than anything else, America is an idea, and, as such, its flourishing depends upon an educated populace, especially with regard to liberty.

Unlike tribal blood ties, American philosophical bonds depend upon teaching and learning about freedom. Properly conceived, Americanism transcends tribalism by enabling all who wish to count themselves as Americans—regardless of ethnicity or creed—to join the Freedom Tribe which is America. President Donald Trump stated this vision of Americanism, in his inaugural address, when he said, "It is time to remember that old wisdom our soldiers will never forget: that whether we are black or brown or white, we all bleed the same red blood of patriots, we all enjoy the same glorious freedoms, and we all salute the same great American Flag."

It was Ronald Reagan who reminded his fellow patriots of their history by framing it in this way: "In this country of ours took place the greatest revolution that has ever taken place in the world's history—the only true revolution. Every other revolution simply exchanged one set of rulers for another. But here, for the first time in all the thousands of years of man's relation to man, a little group of men, the Founding Fathers, for the first time, established the idea that you and I had within ourselves the God-given right and ability to determine our own destiny." Reagan also shared these wise words: "Freedom is never more than one generation away from extinction. We didn't pass it to our children in the bloodstream. It must be fought for, protected, and handed on for them to do the same, or one day we will spend our sunset years telling our children and our children's children what it was once like in the United States where men were free."

The American Founders dreamed up the American republic during the Age of Enlightenment. But it must be the dreams of latter-day Americans that fuel and renew this shared American Dream in the present and into the future. I am one such latter-day American Dreamer. And I hope the readers of this book will join me in appreciating, guarding, and teaching the American Dream to others.

Every single lover of liberty is needed to pass the torch of freedom to future generations. All patriots must do their parts to ensure the survival of our free republic by continuing to learn and to teach others, especially our children. Indeed, every freedom-loving American has the God-given power to tip the scale in favor of liberty.

Use your power. Tip the scale. Let freedom ring!

God save the American Dream!
Paul Dowling, American Patriot & Teacher, July 9, 2018

Foreword: Civil Society & Limited Government: Or, Power to the People!

"I own that I am not a friend to a very energetic government. It is always oppressive."
—Thomas Jefferson

"Power tends to corrupt, and absolute power corrupts absolutely." —Lord Acton

<u>Enshrining the Rights God Granted</u>
America is the first country to be created, based not upon tribal ties or political bonds but upon an idea: Liberty! To be an American, one must only subscribe to the notion that every individual has the Natural Right to live life free—free of other people's prejudices and preferences and customs, as enforced by the tyranny of the majority. The Constitution of the United States does not, in or of itself, create any rights. On the contrary, the job of the Constitution is to protect the Natural Rights which pre-existed the institution of government altogether. Natural Rights were, according to America's Founders, created by Nature's God, and the Framers of our constitutional free republic sought only to make sure that these rights were formally recognized and preserved. In the Declaration of Independence, Thomas Jefferson pointed out that human beings "are endowed by their Creator with certain unalienable Rights, that among these are Life, Liberty and the pursuit of Happiness." Unchecked government has a tendency to modify, diminish, and cancel rights, since government power corrupts. It was Lord Acton who said, "Authority that does not exist for Liberty is not authority but force." Thus, government must be established among the people that is limited in its authority and based upon the consent of the governed.

<u>Limits on Government Are Needed for the People to Be Free</u>
The federal government was created by the sovereign states. This is why state popular majorities—as represented by each state's chosen electors—choose the president, rather than a national popular majority. It is also why understanding the Constitution as a restrictive force that protects the rights of individuals and minorities—even as it outlines how the federal government should function—is so vitally important. The Constitution is the original Contract with America; it was written in the language of the American people, and it was meant to be a simple expression of the people's will that any American citizen might pick up and read without having to consult an attorney to understand it. It is the people's tool for restraining government power, not the government's tool to restrain the people. The Founders, in their wisdom, created a republican form of government that protected Natural Rights from the danger of being canceled by means of a democratic majority vote. This is why the Constitution does not mention the word "democracy" even once; after all, freedom is much more important than majority rule. To ensure liberty, individual rights must be protected. Like any contract, its terms cannot be changed legally, without approval by those who are party to it, not even by creative reinterpretation of a judge or judges—although, in reality, the terms of this contract have been violated repeatedly by judicial activists over the years, and almost always to the detriment of the people's liberty.

<u>Keeping Far-Away Prescriptions & Far-Away Agendas at a Distance</u>
Many of the problems resulting from bad government in America, since America's founding, have been the result of too many solutions for local problems being prescribed by far-away legislators and bureaucrats who have their own agendas—agendas that are often incompatible with the provincial goals and purposes of the people who inhabit the diverse sovereign states and their associated counties and townships. Sometimes less is more; less federal governance often translates into more beneficial outcomes in the local people's ability to enact their own solutions that are more flexible and more appropriate to their own regional requirements and concerns.

<u>Avoiding Divisions Among the People</u>
Much of the political divisiveness that exists on a national level could be avoided, if only the Constitution were restored along the lines of its original purposes. Many of the controversial issues which set Americans against each other should not even be playing out on the national stage. The reason is this: health care, public education, welfare programs, labor relations, housing development, energy regulation, environmental issues, and many other government activities that are so hotly debated with regard to government's proper role and scope, are nowhere listed in the Constitution of the United States as Enumerated Powers of the Congress that would allow for federal control or regulation of these domains of enterprise. These issues are properly left to the states, counties, and townships, under the Tenth Amendment: "The powers not delegated to the United States by the Constitution, nor prohibited by it to the States, are reserved to the States respectively, or to the people."

<u>Washington's Cabinet: Reflecting the Constitutional Prescription of Limitation</u>
It was because of the limited scope of national governance that George Washington, when appointing his presidential advisors, restricted himself to nominating a cabinet of what would eventually number only four people: a Secretary of State, a Secretary of the Treasury, a Secretary of War (now referred to as Secretary of Defense), and an Attorney General. These posts were the only ones, as Washington saw it, that were necessary to help the president attend to his responsibilities as chief executive. And a reading of the Enumerated Powers Clause of the Constitution, in Article I, Section 8, would serve to validate the limited scope of legislative government activity with which the chief executive would need to concern himself:

"The Congress shall have Power To lay and collect Taxes, Duties, Imposts and Excises, to pay the Debts and provide for the common Defence and general Welfare of the United States; but all Duties, Imposts and Excises shall be uniform throughout the United States;

"To borrow money on the credit of the United States;

"To regulate Commerce with foreign Nations, and among the several States, and with the Indian Tribes;

"To establish an uniform Rule of Naturalization, and uniform Laws on the subject of Bankruptcies throughout the United States;

"To coin Money, regulate the Value thereof, and of foreign Coin, and fix the Standard of Weights and Measures;

"To provide for the Punishment of counterfeiting the Securities and current Coin of the United States;

"To establish Post Offices and Post Roads;

"To promote the Progress of Science and useful Arts, by securing for limited Times to Authors and Inventors the exclusive Right to their respective Writings and Discoveries;

"To constitute Tribunals inferior to the supreme Court;

"To define and punish Piracies and Felonies committed on the high Seas, and Offenses against the Law of Nations;

"To declare War, grant Letters of Marque and Reprisal, and make Rules concerning Captures on Land and Water;

"To raise and support Armies, but no Appropriation of Money to that Use shall be for a longer Term than two Years;

"To provide and maintain a Navy;

"To make Rules for the Government and Regulation of the land and naval Forces;

"To provide for calling forth the Militia to execute the Laws of the Union, suppress Insurrections and repel Invasions;

"To provide for organizing, arming, and disciplining, the Militia, and for governing such Part of them as may be employed in the Service of the United States, reserving to the States respectively, the Appointment of the Officers, and the Authority of training the Militia according to the discipline prescribed by Congress;

"To exercise exclusive Legislation in all Cases whatsoever, over such District (not exceeding ten Miles square) as may, by Cession of particular States, and the acceptance of Congress, become the Seat of the Government of the United States, and to exercise like Authority over all Places purchased by the Consent of the Legislature of the State in which the Same shall be, for the Erection of Forts, Magazines, Arsenals, dock-Yards, and other needful Buildings;—And

"To make all Laws which shall be necessary and proper for carrying into Execution the foregoing Powers, and all other Powers vested by this Constitution in the Government of the United States, or in any Department or Officer thereof."

<u>"I Walk on Untrodden Ground"</u>
President Washington, as a student of the Constitution, utilized much caution in how he exercised his authority under its aegis. Washington once said, "I walk on untrodden ground. There is scarcely any part of my conduct which may not hereafter be drawn into precedent." So, Washington well knew that, while the cabinet officers he wished to hire were not defined by the Constitution, there was a portion of the Constitution which stated that the president "may require the Opinion in writing, of the principal Officer in each of the executive Departments, upon any subject relating to the Duties of their respective Offices." The offices referred to by the Constitution needed to be established by the president, in line with the governmental powers enumerated by the people in their Constitution. Also, upon signing the Judiciary Act of 1789, Washington established the federal judiciary system along with the office of Attorney General, in accordance with the Constitution's Article III, Section 1, which states that "[t]he judicial Power of the United States, shall be vested in one supreme Court, and in such inferior Courts as the Congress may from time to time ordain and establish."

<u>The Lawyerly Mischief of Judges</u>
A mischievous reading of the Elastic Clause of the Constitution is chief among the reasons for the overgrowth of the federal bureaucracy. This clause is found in the final part of the Enumerated Powers Clause and states that Congress has the power to "make all Laws which shall be necessary and proper for carrying into Execution the foregoing Powers, and all other Powers vested by this Constitution in the Government of the United States, or in any Department or Officer thereof."

The Supreme Court's reading of "necessary and proper," in its 1819 hearing of *McCulloch v. Maryland*, redefined these words to remove their meaning as a restriction on the Congress. The Court remade the legal meaning of "necessary and proper" to mean, instead, that the Congress was actually endowed with an enlargement of power that it had perhaps been too shy to exercise. Chief Justice John Marshall opined about the Necessary and Proper Clause that "it purport[s] to enlarge, not to diminish the powers vested in the government. It purports to be an additional power, not a restriction on those already granted." By writing these words, Justice Marshall reinterpreted the restrictive nature of the Necessary and Proper Clause in a lawyerly way that twisted its application into a considerably more permissive realm of government action.

The Necessary and Proper Cause, as a result of Marshall's rewrite, has often been used in conjunction with the Commerce Clause to provide a Constitutional basis for the passage and enforcement of a plethora of coercive federal laws. For example, during the days of FDR's New Deal reforms, many of the measures being passed were justified as "necessary and proper" with respect to the state's ability to regulate interstate commerce.

<u>Restoring the Constitution: Slaying the Government Leviathan</u>
The federal government has become incredibly large, and, instead of properly serving the public in a more limited capacity, has acted, with increasing frequency as it has grown, to reverse its rightful role and commandeer a more troubling, all-encompassing role in every aspect of

American life. This has fundamentally changed the country, making the citizenry smaller in comparison to the government Leviathan, as well as making the people less free to decide as many matters for themselves. To slay the government Leviathan, or at least to tame it, the people must once again arm themselves with an understanding of the Constitution and the freedom principles upon which it is founded. The economist Friedrich Hayek is famous for having said, "the larger the government, the smaller the citizen." Hayek was right when he said it, and today his words ring truer than ever.

<u>A Constitutional Convention of the States</u>
If the American people ever decide that the time is ripe for a Constitutional Convention, because the Congress refuses to propose much-needed amendments, the Founders provided for the possibility of the sovereign states calling their own convention, per Article Five: "The Congress, whenever two thirds of both Houses shall deem it necessary, shall propose Amendments to this Constitution, or, on the Application of the Legislatures of two thirds of the several States, shall call a Convention for proposing Amendments, which, in either Case, shall be valid to all Intents and Purposes, as Part of this Constitution, when ratified by the Legislatures of three fourths of the several States, or by Conventions in three fourths thereof, as the one or the other Mode of Ratification may be proposed by the Congress."

The purpose of such a convention would traditionally be to propose clarifications to the limitations on government power as formal amendments to the Constitution, thereby putting teeth back into the Necessary and Proper Clause as a restrictive force and limiting the use of the Commerce Clause, among other corrective actions that the people might deem appropriate. This would restore the power of the sovereign states to solve most political problems themselves, thus keeping issues that are best remedied closer to the people from dividing the entire nation.

<u>The Constitution Is the Center of Discourse</u>
The Constitution is the center of discourse in America. It reflects the will of the people and remains the people's Instrument to restrain government force. It is the great leveler, since any change or addition to the Constitution must be according to the will of the people at large. And the continuance of the Constitution in America today demonstrates the fact that efforts to typify it as being more in the service of one or another political ideology is entirely counterfactual, or else the American people would reject the freedom offered by the Constitution as the center of proper political debate in America. As long as freedom is America's creed, political success, in fair elections, will belong to those who embrace the people and their values, which are based upon Natural Rights and all the liberty that such rights imply.

Thus far, America is still a land where the people govern, although it seems to be less and less the case each year, as the state grows in size and the rights of the people diminish. This is largely the result of the cessation of accurate teaching about the Constitution and the principles that inform it. It is time for the American people to take the Constitution more seriously than they have been and to renew their understanding and appreciation of it. Learning about the Constitution is the only way to set the conditions for success with respect to decreasing the size of the state and increasing the size of the people's liberty once again.

<u>Helping the People Take Back Their Power: Factoring In Authorial Intent</u>
It is the hope of this author that this book will help in the effort to educate people about the intents and purposes of the Constitution. The functions of the Constitution are broken down and described in brief, but, perhaps more importantly, there is a concerted effort to explain the most important principles informing the Instrument. Appendices are meant to be read, like the chapters of most books, but they may be read in any order (which is why they are being called appendices). The purpose of this text is to offer a short, readable work that is broken down into easily digestible units. The full text of the Constitution, its Bill of Rights, and the remaining seventeen amendments can be found in appendices G, H, and I. The original document without amendments (in Appendix G) is 4,440 words in length. Other appendices explain and elaborate the importance of certain God-given Natural Rights, and there is also an appendix about America's First Principles (Appendix J) that explains a good deal with regard to the belief system of the founding generation (and thus the basis for the "operating system" of America's Golden-Rule-based Constitution). Enjoy learning about this exciting topic!

Introduction: Dispelling Misconceptions About the Founders & the Constitution

"Proclaim LIBERTY throughout all the land unto all the inhabitants thereof."
—Leviticus 25:10

<u>A Too-Rare Occurrence: Leading a Constitution Club in a Public School</u>
I have been a teacher for three decades and have witnessed the conversion of many schools from education institutions to indoctrination centers. Many teachers these days depict America's Founders as "dead, racist white guys" whose ideas are unworthy of any respect or consideration. The Constitution is taught, wrongly, as bigoted and sexist, while America's Founding Fathers are generally typified as racist and even anti-gay, but these statements are unfair.

So I formed a Constitution Club at my school to dispel the misrepresentations that disciples of the collectivist ideology of democratic socialism are daily feeding our students. Socialism is nowadays quite often labeled "social justice" and is about calling upon each individual to be "fair" to the socialist collective by submitting to the will of the majority in all matters, rather than limiting the power of the collective and obligating a civil society to be fair to every individual. This is almost never explained to students, who are often persuaded to support some rather bad ideas—all in the name of "social justice"—that only end up empowering the collective majority to force its will upon the supporters of individual rights. What students need to be taught is that their rights are best preserved not by joining with a political majority to "win" protections they already possess under the Constitution, but by defending the rights of all individuals. Ayn Rand once said, "Do not make the mistake of the ignorant who think that an individualist is a man who says: 'I'll do as I please at everybody else's expense.' An individualist is a man who recognizes the inalienable individual rights of man—his own and those of others."

Before I could get students to attend my Constitution Club meetings, I had to overcome objections from three campus groups: the black student group, the feminist men and women, and the lesbian/gay support group. Their objections, considering what they were being fed by the enthusiasts of so-called "social justice," were understandable. But their objections were easily overcome by the teaching of accurate, historical facts about our founding documents and our Founding Fathers, something schools are seldom doing nowadays. Even areas of the country that are more traditional in outlook are suffering from the fact that the college graduates who are staffing the public schools are almost universally being graduated from socialist universities who practice political indoctrination. It is the same problem Americans are seeing in the propensity of many district attorneys to prosecute defenders of innocent life who defend themselves against criminal assault in their own homes by means of using firearms; new attorneys being hired by townships and cities across America are graduating from socialist institutions, and their understanding of individual rights can be much different than the traditional, freedom-based notions that Constitutionalists hold.

<u>Black Students: Learning About the Anti-Slavery Clause</u>
Article I, Section 2, of the Constitution contains a clause known as the 3/5 Clause, or the Anti-Slavery Clause. It reads as follows: "Representatives and direct Taxes shall be apportioned among the several States which may be included within this Union, according to their respective Numbers, which shall be determined by adding to the whole Number of free Persons, including those bound to Service for a Term of Years [Indentured Servants], and excluding Indians not taxed, three fifths of all other Persons [who are unfree]."

The reason this clause exists is to encourage slave states to free their slaves by making their representation in the House of Representatives increase upon the actual freeing of them. Any teaching that the Founders thought of black persons as only 3/5 a human being is false. It should also be pointed out that there is no consideration of race in this clause. The Constitution is color-blind with respect to race. In fact, more than 20% of slaveholders in the South, at the time of the American Civil War, were African-American freemen. And black abolitionists, such as Frederick Douglass, simply wanted the Constitution applied to blacks in the same way that it was being applied to whites; nobody was in favor of abandoning the Constitution.

<u>Feminist Students: Learning the Truth About Equal Suffrage for Women</u>
Article I, Section 4, Clause One, of the Constitution reads as follows: "The Times, Places and Manner of holding Elections for Senators and Representatives, shall be prescribed in each State by the Legislature thereof. . . ." There is actually nothing in the gender-neutral language of the Constitution that states that women cannot vote. All voting-eligibility rules are left to the states to decide.

By the time the Nineteenth Amendment was ratified, in August of 1920, twenty-seven states already allowed women to vote in presidential elections. The Nineteenth Amendment sped up the process of giving this right to all American women; but the point being made here is that the Constitution itself was indeed written to be gender-neutral. This is why women in some states were able to gain voting rights prior to 1920.

The Nineteenth Amendment reads like this: "Section 1. The right of the citizens of the United States to vote shall not be denied or abridged by the United States or by any State on account of sex. Section 2. Congress shall have power to enforce this article by appropriate legislation."

A brief note on gender neutrality in the Constitution: In Standard English, the pronouns "he" and "him" are gender-neutral pronouns when they refer to persons of unknown gender or when the gender of persons referred to is not meant to be specified. (Even in scripture, God is rendered gender-neutral by being referred to as "He.") There was no alternative grammatical convention in use in the day of the Founders. The same convention exists today, in English and in other modern languages. Bilingual students comprehend this convention with ease.

<u>Lesbian & Gay Students: Learning About Washington's Tolerance of Homosexuality</u>
Our Founders lived in the era called the Enlightenment, and the value of tolerance was held in

high esteem. General George Washington, during the American Revolutionary War, employed the services of a Prussian military officer by the name of Friedrich von Steuben (pronounced "Freedrikh fohn Shtoyben"). Washington hired him to train his soldiers in superior Prussian methods of warfare, to instill new confidence into the rag-tag outfit. Washington also had von Steuben write the first military training manual for America's armed forces.

Baron von Steuben had been discharged from the Prussian military, due to his "affections for members of his own sex," despite his reputation as a military genius. Fleeing imprisonment, he ended up in France interviewing with American ambassador Benjamin Franklin for a job in Washington's army. Dr. Franklin decided that von Steuben's military expertise trumped any consideration of the homosexual issue and that tolerance was called for.

Washington valued von Steuben as a friend and associate and never spoke with indiscretion of von Steuben's personal affairs, nor did he write about them in any official or private documents or letters. George Washington, the Father of Our Country—through his tolerance and encouragement of an outcast military genius—made Friedrich von Steuben, a gay man, the Father of Our Country's Armed Forces.

<u>America's Ever-Unfolding Promissory Note</u>
Whatever their shortcomings, our Founders understood they were not perfect. They knew, however, that even an imperfect birth of freedom would provide America with the opportunity for a great and unending experiment. The blueprint for this experiment in individual liberty, that they wrote into the US Constitution, would provide its inheritors with an ever-unfolding promissory note for the sustenance and enlargement of life, liberty, and the pursuit of happiness throughout the ages.

The Constitution our Founders bestowed upon us is written in a neutral style, without specific references to race or gender. President Reagan referred to America's constitutional republic as a "shining city on a hill" and the "last best hope for man on earth." If we want those words to remain true, that promissory note must be jealously protected for every generation yet to come.

Why a Free Republic Is Necessary for Life, Liberty, & the Pursuit of Happiness

"Democracy is two wolves and a sheep voting on what's for dinner. Liberty is a well-armed lamb contesting the vote." —Attributed to Benjamin Franklin

A Republic . . . If You Can Keep It
It was September 18, 1787, as Ben Franklin, emerging from Independence Hall at the close of the Constitutional Convention, was accosted by a curious Mrs. Powel. "Well, Doctor," the woman queried, "what have we got, a republic or a monarchy?"

"A republic, madam," Dr. Franklin replied, "if you can keep it."

Benjamin Franklin, who was 81 years of age, knew full well that it would be up to the American people to take care that they elect wise and upright leaders, in order for the Constitution to endure. Leaders of good character and strong moral fiber, who would respect the limits imposed by the Constitution, would be needed for American freedom to continue into the future. While the Constitution clearly promises limited government, it takes leaders with integrity to keep that promise.

Why Life in a Republic Is Preferable to Life in a Democracy
A republic (Latin: *res publica* = people's thing or public matter) is a form of government in which governance is considered the "people's thing"—a matter for the public to direct. The executive power is not above the law and may only execute the laws, not make them. All state officials are either elected or appointed by elected officials. In contrast to a democracy, which is Majority Unlimited, a republic is Majority Limited, protecting the rights of every individual person, every minority group, against the majority. Every citizen of a republic possesses Natural Rights that no majority has the legal authority to infringe or abolish. So, America is a republic, not a democracy. The word "democracy" is never mentioned within the text of the Constitution; this is a point that cannot be overemphasized.

The Republican Principle Promotes Liberty for All
The Republican Principle is this: **Freedom is more important than Majority Rule.**
A republic legally restrains the whims and prejudices of the majority from harming the individual.

The Democratic Principle Permits Tyranny of the Mob
The Democratic Principle is this: **Majority Rule is more important than Freedom.**
A democracy legally permits the whims and prejudices of the majority to harm the individual.

Freedom Means Power to the People
A free republic uses a constitutional framework to fence off the Natural Rights of the people, so

they may not be violated by policy or by law. This means that certain kinds of rules are illegal to make. Therefore, in the United States, a law that infringes the freedom of speech is illegal and will not stand; likewise, a law that bars one from being permitted arms in a fight with a criminal assailant is off-limits; and so is any law that allows spurious police-state searches of a person's property or prevents freedom of association or other important freedoms. In a free republic, the burden of proof is on the government to show there is probable cause to conduct a search or to file a criminal charge, and the government must prove criminal misconduct beyond a shadow of a doubt before imprisoning an individual, since every person has the right to be presumed innocent until proven guilty—and accusations are never proof of wrongdoing.

Because the majority is not allowed to make certain kinds of rules, individuals and minorities enjoy legal protections against any and all ill-informed prejudices of the mob. Freedom is considered more important than majority rule in a free republic, whereas, in a socialist democracy, the majority can make whatever rules it wishes against minorities and individuals, which is why so many elitist oligarchies and dictatorships rise to power in democratically-elected governments that are not limited by the fencing-off of individual rights, in accordance with republican principles. Natural Rights are important: with Natural Rights, freedom reigns, and the people govern; without Natural Rights, tyranny rules, and the people groan. Without the retention of Natural Rights by the people, the government assumes sole power to grant rights as privileges. And these privileges are all politically determined, such as Hitler's issuing of the privilege to own a gun for self-defense only to fellow National Socialists. One of the first priorities of socialists like Hitler is the confiscation of all weaponry owned by individuals and minorities who are not in sympathy with the goals of socialism.

<u>So, What Is a Natural Right?</u>
A Natural Right is something that one is naturally permitted to do independently for oneself with the reasonable expectation that no person and no state entity will impede one from doing it: speaking one's mind, defending oneself and one's loved ones from harm, minding one's own business upon one's own property, deciding how one wishes to make a living, peaceably gathering with whatever group of people one wishes to spend time with. . . .

In a republic, all human beings possess the same rights—which means that government agents are not allowed to exercise rights that the citizenry does not possess—and one must not violate someone else's rights in order to procure a good or service. In other words, a man has the right to hire a doctor to examine his children, but if he must take money (a form of property) from a third party, by threat of force at gunpoint (via government taxation), in order to pay for those medical services, then he has violated someone else's property rights in order to obtain those services for himself; or if he compel the physician to examine or treat his family, by using physical force against the physician, then he has directly violated the right of the medical professional to determine his own actions, free from coercion.

One has the right to work to earn money to purchase healthcare, and one has the right to barter for medical services by providing services to a doctor in exchange for his. But the minute taxes are collected to pay for services for which not all members of the general public derive equal benefit, then the general welfare is not being promoted, only some individuals' welfare at the expense of other individuals; this is wrongful taxation, because some people are being harmed by having their rights violated, so that others may receive a special privilege not being offered in equal measure to all persons taxed. A free people must always keep in mind that government depends on force; although some government is needed to keep people from harming one another, government should not be facilitating harm by infringing the people's Natural Rights.

<u>Private Property: Without It, There Is No Individual Freedom</u>
All crimes are crimes against property. Slavery is perhaps the worst crime short of murder. And it is a crime against property, since one's person is one's first and most intimate property. Therefore, the theft of a person's labor—even if perpetrated by the state—is a crime against property. The fruit of one's labor is one's property; thus, forced confiscation of any portion of the fruit of a person's labor for purposes unavailable to him is a violation of Natural Rights. Every crime is, at its root, an act of theft: murder is stealing a life; slavery is stealing someone's labor; and taxation for purposes unrelated to the general welfare is a form of stealing. Creation of a law that makes self-defense illegal is stealing the rights of potential victims to enjoy equal protection of their lives, along with the criminals who wish to harm them. Pure democracy is, therefore, a constant risk to life and limb, since a simple majority vote can wipe away all fairness with regard to the needs of individuals and minorities to protect themselves by legal right.

A republican state is extremely limited in its ability to convert rights into privileges and, therefore, is safer for the people. Since a constitutional republic creates an even playing field—rather than allowing the kind of rule-making that gives all the advantages to people who refuse to follow rules altogether—people have the power to limit evil interference by use of the same weapons that criminal assailants have at their disposal. This is an important Natural Right for the people to retain, for, without it, all crimes are not only enabled, but encouraged—including the possibility of corrupt politicians' criminal acts against the citizenry in ways against which there would be no recourse to act as a check upon their criminality.

The right to protect private property is necessary for citizens of a republic to enjoy the Natural Right to protect themselves against criminal behavior—whether that be against the criminal activities of a single individual or of a collective entity, including a tyrannical state. And if there be no right to protect property—and thereby no right to protect one's own physical person—then the most basic rights to life, liberty, and the pursuit of happiness cannot be guaranteed, except by special consideration of the state, in the name of the collective majority. Such collectivist governance cancels individual rights and the superior position of the individual to the state, thereby spoiling the protection of Natural Rights and personal freedoms that a republic has to offer*.

———

*See Appendix A on the Battle of Athens, Tennessee, to see why the right to keep and bear arms, a Natural Right protected for the free people of a republic, acts as an insurance policy against tyranny.

"The state of nature has a law of nature to govern it, which obliges every one: and reason, which is that law, teaches all mankind, who will but consult it, that being all equal and independent, no one ought to harm another in his life, health, liberty, or possessions . . . [and] when his own preservation comes not in competition, ought he, as much as he can, to preserve the rest of mankind, and may not, unless it be to do justice on an offender, take away, or impair the life, or what tends to the preservation of the life, the liberty, health, limb, or goods of another." —John Locke, in The Second Treatise on Civil Government

"Freedom is not a gift bestowed upon us by other men, but a right that belongs to us by the laws of God and Nature." —Benjamin Franklin

<u>Republicanism in Action: Respecting the People's Natural Rights</u>
The wise representatives of the American people who framed the Constitution believed in Natural Laws that governed human nature. These Americans understood that human beings possessed Natural Rights that could not be taken away from them. These Unalienable Rights include the following: the right to worship and live according to one's own conscience; the right to speak one's mind freely; the right to defend one's life, liberty, and property from danger; the right to petition the government to right any wrongs it has committed against the people; the right to free association; the right to publish one's opinions without restraint; the right to travel freely; the right to live privately without unwarranted government inference; the right to be judged by one's peers and not the government.

Since the new government would be of the people, by the people, and for the people, the government would *not* have the right to do those things which would be wrong for the people to do. The government would exist only for doing those things which the people have the right to do, but could not easily do as individuals. The people created the government and, therefore, had the right to restrain it. The people were in charge of the government, and not the other way around.

<u>A Free Republic: The People Come First, Not the State</u>
The people can only delegate powers to the government that they rightly possess themselves. Thus, the people institute government to protect what is natural to the people that predates government altogether; the government does not grant rights as a list of privileges that they might decide, at some point, to withdraw.

Indeed, the French political theorist Frédéric Bastiat writes, in *The Law*: "Life, liberty, and property do not exist because men have made laws. On the contrary, it was the fact that life, liberty, and property existed beforehand that caused men to make laws in the first place." The people are thus superior to government and must ensure that government remains subservient, lest an unnatural despotism develop.

<u>Republican Principles: The Principle of Agency & the Principle of Equal Protection</u>
Government should operate based upon a set of consistently applied universal principles, rather than upon fleeting popular notions. One such principle, the **Principle of Agency**, holds that government, as the people's agent, is only permitted to do what the people are permitted to do. This form of governance fundamentally validates the subservient relationship of the government to the people. It means that government does not rightly possess any power to harm one individual or group in order to help another individual or group, without **Due Process** and **Equal Protection**, according to laws that respect the Natural, God-given Rights of the people.

<u>Republicanism to the Rescue: Individual Rights Must Be Respected by the Majority</u>
Democracy, without any republican form of Equal Protection, can often prove destructive, if not outright tyrannical. Only a system in which each person has Equal Protection works to ensure liberty and justice for everyone. In a popular example, a horse thief is caught by a posse of 31 people. A member of the posse shouts, "Let's hang him from a tree!" A vote is held, and 16 vote to hang the horse thief. In a democracy, the horse thief is hanged, and that is the end.

In a republic, however, the sheriff calls out, "You can't hang him! He has his rights." The Golden Rule is invoked: "You would want a chance to explain why you stole a horse, so this man gets a chance to explain. He'll have his day in court." This fleshing out of the Golden Rule, called the Right to Due Process, means that judgment is withheld until after a full hearing of all evidence has taken place. Due Process is what guarantees Equal Protection.

Perhaps the man stole the horse as a result of having been threatened, or maybe he mistook the horse for his own. His side of the story must be heard. It is his right. Safety and freedom are both promoted when the Right to Due Process is enforced.

The sheriff from the story was legitimately hired to protect the lives and property of the people, because the people already possessed the Natural Right to protect their own lives and property. So the delegation of this power to an agent who might act on the people's behalf was right and proper. It is also fitting that the sheriff enforce justice according to the Golden Rule, making sure the people do not treat the accused in any way that they would hate to be treated.

<u>The Golden Rule</u>
Much has been said about the Judeo-Christian **Golden Rule**, with regard to how the Constitution embodies a set of principles which is largely based upon it. Perhaps the strongest formulation of the Golden Rule, to which Western Culture adheres, is Hillel's statement: "Do not do unto others that which you hate done unto yourself." This way of stating the rule is the most compassionate, because "Love your neighbor as yourself" (*Leviticus 19:18*) or "Do unto others as you would have them do unto you" (*Matthew 7:12*) are positively stated, meaning that any action that a given individual enjoys experiencing—even a masochistic or painful one—is all right for that individual to do to others. The negative formulation is wiser, since it commands an individual to refrain from doing all things unpleasant to that individual

"The smallest minority on earth is the individual. Those who deny individual rights cannot claim to be defenders of minorities." —Ayn Rand

"Government is not reason; it is not eloquence; it is force. Like fire, it is a dangerous servant and a fearful master." —Attributed to George Washington

<u>Without Freedom, There Are No Rights</u>
To make sure that the power of the government remains restricted, a system of checks and balances is needed to protect freedom. This system makes the government less efficient in its exercise of power, but more effective in protecting the rights and freedoms of individuals. The authentic power of the individual rests entirely in the individual's right to act freely and in the government's obligation to restrain itself. Without the freedom to act according to one's own conscience, to express what is on one's mind, whether it be offensive or inoffensive, there can be no Natural Right to think or act out of one's own preferences. When the majority can veto one's freedom of expression, one is living in a world of group-think socialism and government force. As the Founders of the American republic well knew, government rules always hold the potential of having to be enforced at gunpoint. In the end, government is force, which means that, for the purposes of a free republic, the best government is that which governs least.

<u>Co-Equal Frustration in Governance</u>
According to the founding principles of the American republic, three co-equal branches share the responsibility of running the government. Each branch exists to provide necessary checks on the exercise of power by the other branches. This is to prevent any one person or group of people in the government from becoming too powerful. It also forces more agreement across greater numbers of people to occur, before a law can be enacted, changed, or repealed. The framers of the Constitution much preferred "gridlock" to a state of affairs where an efficient government might too easily pass laws that eventually turn out not to be good for the American people. No change at all is generally preferable to the making of a poor choice when it comes to new law. And the most agreement possible among people and their representatives is generally better than a bare majority. Liberty must be protected at every turn, so frustrating politicians' efforts, by design, in order to guarantee a slower and more deliberate process is preferable to making change too easy to come by.

"They define a republic to be a government of laws, and not of men." —*John Adams*

<u>"We the People": The Entire Focus of a Constitutional Republic</u>
The Preamble to the Constitution reads as follows: "We the People of the United States, in Order to form a more perfect Union, establish Justice, insure domestic Tranquility, provide for the common defence, promote the general Welfare, and secure the Blessings of Liberty to ourselves and our Posterity, do ordain and establish this Constitution for the United States of America."*

Short and to the point, the Constitution says in its opening statement that it is the American people who give license to the new government. The reasons mentioned for writing this social contract are as follows: enforcement of just laws, defense of the nation, use of funds only for things of benefit to everyone, and a limitation on government power in order to promote freedom for all into the future. The Constitution is really about the rule of law, with equal treatment for all, and for the benefit of everyone—not the rule of those who would otherwise create division among citizens, then grant special favors to the larger half of them in order to procure the favor of their support in return. Also, it must be pointed out that no one in office—in the legislative, executive, or judicial branches—is above the law.

———

*Author's Note: As a teacher, I have always taught the Preamble by making one editorial change in punctuation to aid comprehension. Since the Preamble possesses so many commas, I have found it helpful to change the first and final commas to hyphens, according to modern usage, in order to give visual clarity to the Founders' intended meaning: "We the People of the United States—in Order to form a more perfect Union, establish Justice, insure domestic Tranquility, provide for the common defence, promote the general Welfare, and secure the Blessings of Liberty to ourselves and our Posterity—do ordain and establish this Constitution for the United States of America."

Article I

"The members of the legislative department . . . are numerous. They are distributed and dwell among the people at large. Their connections of blood, of friendship, and of acquaintance embrace a great proportion of the most influential part of the society . . . they are more immediately the confidential guardians of their rights and liberties." —James Madison

"We the People" Must Come First
The Constitution first establishes the legislative branch of government—called Congress—in Article I, based on the premise that "We the People" must stand in importance before all other matters. It is the American people who, by Natural Right, make the laws, not the president and not the judiciary. The legislative branch of government is bicameral, meaning it is divided into two chambers: the House of Representatives and the Senate.

The House delegation of each state is set according to the proportional number of inhabitants each state holds of the overall population. Every state is guaranteed to have at least one representative, no matter how small its population might be. Members of the House must stand for re-election every two years.

The Senate delegation of each state numbers exactly two per state, so that each state shares equally in its representation. A senator holds a six-year term of office, one third of the Senate standing for re-election every two years.

The Congress possesses only a limited number of Enumerated Powers, per Section 8 of Article I. In order to protect the freedom of the people, the Congress is supposed to keep to these specific areas of influence, lest the legislative branch become too strong and begin usurping the power of the people, the municipalities, the counties, and the states.*

Honorable Mention: The Anti-Slavery Clause, Which Is Often Mistaught, Begs for Clarification
Perhaps Article I, Section 2, of the Constitution bears mentioning here, for the purpose of elucidation with regard to its meaning, since it contains a clause known as the 3/5 Clause, or the Anti-Slavery Clause, which is widely misunderstood and therefore often suffers from being mischaracterized when taught. The clause states the following: "Representatives and direct Taxes shall be apportioned among the several States which may be included within this Union, according to their respective Numbers, which shall be determined by adding to the whole Number of free Persons, including those bound to Service for a Term of Years [Indentured Servants], and excluding Indians not taxed, three fifths of all other Persons [who are unfree]." This clause might be reworded as follows: "Congressional representation and direct taxation is to be divided among the states according to the whole number of free persons, including indentured servants and three-fifths of all other persons, but excluding Indians who do not pay taxes."

The reason for the existence of the clause is to encourage slave states to free their slaves by making their representation in the House of Representatives increase upon the actual freeing of them. Slaveholders in the Southern states actually wanted each slave to count as an entire person, while Northern abolitionists wanted each slave to count zero in the census until freed. It is not even rational to believe any argument that says abolitionists thought of black slaves as *not* being human, while Southern slave owners thought of them as *fully* human. The 3/5 language was a compromise, not a statement by anyone that black slaves are only worth 3/5 a human being, a fallacy that is often promoted by inaccurate teaching in America's schools. Also, any teaching that the Founders wrote race into the Constitution is completely false. There is no consideration of race, even in the Anti-Slavery Clause; the only consideration is of "free persons" versus "other persons." The Constitution is entirely color-blind with respect to race. It is also true, although generally overlooked by uncaring and counterfactual researchers, that many Southerners were themselves abolitionists just as some Northern slave merchants were not. It is even true that Thomas Jefferson, himself a slave owner, was against slavery and worked his entire adult life to end the Peculiar Institution**.

<u>The Truth About Equal Suffrage for Women</u>
When it comes to voting rights, there is actually nothing in the gender-neutral language of the Constitution that says that women may not vote. And, according to Article I, Section 4, voting-eligibility rules are left to the states and to the people: : "The Times, Places and Manner of holding Elections for Senators and Representatives, shall be prescribed in each State by the Legislature thereof. . . ."

By the time the Nineteenth Amendment to the Constitution was ratified, in August of 1920, twenty-seven states were already allowing women to vote in presidential elections. Since most states were permitting women to vote, before the Nineteenth Amendment was passed, the amendment was not as controversial as many might imagine. There were, however, some states that were slow to change, so the amendment process did speed up the awarding of this right to all American women.

The Nineteenth Amendment reads like this: "Section 1. The right of the citizens of the United States to vote shall not be denied or abridged by the United States or by any State on account of sex. Section 2. Congress shall have power to enforce this article by appropriate legislation."

A brief note on gender neutrality in the Constitution that bears not only mentioning but repeating: In traditional English, the pronouns "he," "him," and "his" are gender-neutral when referring to persons of unknown or unspecified gender. (This is also true of references to God as "He.") There was no other grammar rule or custom in use in the day of the Founders. The same convention exists today, in Standard English as well as in other modern languages. Bilingual speakers comprehend this concept with ease.

<u>*Habeas Corpus*: Does the Power to Suspend this Right Belong to the Congress or the President?</u>
President Lincoln came under criticism, due to his suspension of *Habeas Corpus*, during his first few months in office. *Habeas Corpus* is Latin for "that you have the body." It is the right to be released by a captor—usually a sheriff, a warden, or some other state agent—so that one's

physical body may be brought in front of a judge, to determine whether or not there exists any legitimate authority to continue holding the prisoner in physical custody. This is usually accomplished by having a *Writ of Habeas Corpus* issued that carries the weight of a court order.

Lincoln was inaugurated on March 4, 1861, and was already calling Congress into special session three days after the Confederates' April 12th attack on Fort Sumter to prevent the resupply of the fort with foodstuffs. It was during the interval of waiting for Congress to convene that Lincoln suspended the privilege of the *Writ of Habeas Corpus*, which is allowed under the Suspension Clause of the US Constitution, per Article I, Section 9, Clause Two: "The privilege of the *Writ of Habeas Corpus* shall not be suspended, unless when in Cases of Rebellion or Invasion the public Safety may require it." Lincoln's claim was that he did so as commander-in-chief of the armed forces during an inarguable time of rebellion, and his Constitutional concerns prompted him to address the Congress on the selfsame day Congress convened, on July 4, 1861, in order to be sure that, as an Article I provision, it was placed in the hands of the legislative branch as soon as possible.

Concerning his April 27th suspension of the *Writ* on part of the Florida coast, and his July 2nd order authorizing suspension of the *Writ* between Philadelphia and New York, Lincoln gave the justification that "we have a case of rebellion, and the public safety does require" the use of that [suspension] clause. Lincoln continued: "Now it is insisted that Congress, and not the Executive, is vested with this power [since the Suspension Clause is in Article I, which describes the powers of Congress]. But the Constitution itself is silent as to which, or who, is to exercise the power; and as the provision was plainly made for a dangerous emergency, it cannot be believed the Framers of the Instrument [the Constitution] intended that, in every case, the danger should run its course, until Congress could be called together; the very assembling of which might be prevented . . . by the rebellion. . . . Whether there shall be any legislation upon the subject, and if any, what, is submitted entirely to the better judgment of Congress." Congress, in taking no immediate action, thereby allowed Lincoln's action to stand without criticism, although Congress eventually did give sanction to Lincoln's use of the Suspension Clause, by legislative action, on March 3, 1863.

Lincoln's argument as to why he did not wait for Congress was accepted, although technically the power to suspend the *Writ* lies firmly within the power of the Congress to invoke. Lincoln's emergency use of the power in a time of rebellion was forgiven by the Congress in that one instance, but this does not mean that the power properly belongs to the president without any oversight whatsoever by the people's representatives. By eventually passing a law to suspend *Habeas Corpus*, per Lincoln's belated request, the Congress affirmed itself as the proper authority, per the Constitution, to invoke the Suspension Clause. By not complaining about the president's invocation of the suspension, the Congress merely allowed for the imperfect sensibilities of the moment. After all, Article IV, Section 4, Clause Two, of the Constitution states that the United States "shall protect each of them [States of the Union] against Invasion; and on Application of the Legislature, or of the Executive (when the Legislature cannot be convened), against domestic Violence." Lincoln may have found the language of Article IV,

Section 4, to be a support to his reasoning that, just because "the Legislature cannot be convened," the Executive is not relieved of his responsibility to "protect each of them [the States of the Union] against Invasion."

______

*See Appendix G in order to read Articles I through VII of the US Constitution.
**See Appendix K for a more detailed account of Jefferson's fight to ban slavery.

Article II

"When a man assumes a public trust, he should consider himself as public property."
—Thomas Jefferson

<u>The Chief Executive Is There for the People's Purposes</u>
Article II of the Constitution creates the executive branch. The chief executive who must "take care that the laws be faithfully executed" is the President of the United States. Although the presidency can prove to be quite a powerful office, especially if the leader holding it were to possess the power to persuade, the President of the United States, in point of fact, holds only six formal duties: 1) commander-in-chief of the armed forces; 2) chief executive of the bureaucracy; 3) chief-of-state for all Americans; 4) chief diplomat in handling foreign relations; 5) chief architect for necessary legislation; 6) the conscience of the nation, with the power to grant pardons and reprieves where justice demands it. The President of the United States may stand for re-election after four years in office and may serve for only two terms. The President of the United States holds the power to approve legislation by his signature or to disapprove it by his veto. The Congress may, however, override a presidential veto upon a two-thirds vote of both chambers, thus affirming the law and putting it into effect above the objections of the president.

<u>Electing the President While Protecting the Rights of the Minority</u>
Also in Article II is the system of electing the president, by choosing Electors to vote in the Electoral College, which was created with special consideration given to small states. The number of Electors is determined by adding the number of representatives to the number of senators for any given state. Thus, Rhode Island receives three electoral votes, rather than one; 1/435 would be the ratio of representation if a direct-proportion model were used; but Rhode Island is represented within the Electoral College at a ratio of 3/535—which is significantly better, giving such a small state more power in a close election. The impact of this on larger states is one of diminishing their power to bully smaller ones. Thus, to succeed to office, a presidential candidate must win many statewide popular-vote majorities, rather than relying on a national popular-vote majority that could be easily tipped by a heavy turnout in a few homogenous population centers. Another way of looking at it is this: The Electoral College system protects the rights of the minority against the majority*, by ensuring that smaller states have a legal means of resisting the will of larger states in close elections; the Electoral College also acts as a safeguard against one state's voter fraud having widespread impact, since one state cannot—either wittingly or unwittingly—fraudulently decide the entire presidential election on its own, simply by having permitted a large number of illegal ballots to be cast.

<u>The Imperial Presidential Bureaucracy</u>
One criticism of the US Presidency has been that it has grown too much in power over the years, to the extent that the president can accomplish many of his goals relatively unchecked. As the size of the executive-branch bureaucracy has grown, with its ability to write an endless number of rules on its own, without the ability of the people's representatives to oversee them all effectively, the president has become empowered to take on a role uncomfortably close to that of

23

being a lawgiver in many instances. Such an imperial presidency does not comply with the Founders' vision that the people's representatives write all the rules and that the chief executive enforce them. This bureaucracy-based executive *fiat* is known as "administrative law."

Executive Orders
Executive orders are not mentioned in the US Constitution, so they do not vest the chief executive with any special duty or power. They are merely clarifications of policy that are within the legal discretion of the president to direct. Under George Washington, such orders were known as proclamations—such as President Washington's proclamation, at the behest of Congress, that a national day of thanksgiving be proclaimed; appropriately, Washington urged the American people, on October 3, 1789, to celebrate Thursday, November 26, 1789, as a day of thanksgiving. No law was violated by anyone who chose not to honor the day. The executive order was first called by its modern name in 1862, during Abraham Lincoln's presidency. Executive orders, memos, and other actions by the president must fall within the law as written by the Congress. An executive order is not allowed, Constitutionally-speaking, to take on the status of a new law. There have been issues in the past with the use of executive orders, and other acts of executive *fiat*, to usurp the Congressional role of making and repealing laws. A favorite means by which the executive might illegitimately act to functionally change a law, by circumventing Congress with an executive order, is to invoke "prosecutorial discretion" before announcing what class of criminal is not to be prosecuted. This is an improper distortion of presidential power, where the president's duty to "take care that the laws be faithfully executed" is viewed as discretionary by those practicing the use of executive *fiat* to effect legal changes.

Restoring Constitutional Restraint by Reducing the Size of the Executive Branch
One surefire way to scale back the overweening power of the executive would be to enforce the Tenth Amendment, eliminating all executive-branch departments that do not specifically fall within the Enumerated Powers of the federal government. In other words, since the Congress is not empowered by the Constitution to make laws about education or medicine or energy, the executive departments writing rules for those areas should not exist. Congress should not be passing laws in areas not enumerated by the Constitution as being under its authority, and the executive should not have departments organized for enforcing such un-Constitutional laws and writing rules to go with them. The sovereign states need to be in charge of creating such laws and rules, rather than having their powers usurped by the executive, in conjunction with the legislative, branch.

------

*See more on how the Electoral College places freedom above democracy, in Appendix B.

Article III

"Justice, and only justice, shall you pursue, so that you may live and possess the land the Lord your God is giving you." —Deuteronomy 16:20

<u>"Justice, & Only Justice, Shall You Pursue"</u>
The judicial branch finds its origin in Article III of the Constitution. The Supreme Court has jurisdiction in ten special circumstances to hear cases. (Originally, there were eleven, but these were reduced to ten by the Eleventh Amendment to the Constitution.) The Supreme Court, according to the Constitution, is to function as the court of final appeal for the federal court system. Jurists of the Supreme Court serve non-expiring terms, so long as they maintain good behavior. This means they are insulated from having to answer to voters for their decisions and are free to rule on the law, without worry as to whether a verdict is politically popular or not.

<u>*Marbury v. Madison*</u>
In 1803, in a case called *Marbury v. Madison*, the Supreme Court ruled that it had the sole right of judicial review to determine whether a law is Constitutional or un-Constitutional. As written, the Constitution vests no such exclusive power in the Supreme Court, even if the Court would like to maintain otherwise. The Congress and the President of the United States have just as much to say about such matters as the Supreme Court does. And, ultimately, the American people have the final say on issues with regard to their Constitutionality. There is no language in the Constitution that allows any court in the United States—even the Supreme Court—to rule into being a special power for itself.

Yet today, most Americans think of the nine justices on the Supreme Court as the only proper judges of what is Constitutional and what is not. This is a fallacious situation that could change, if only the legislative and executive branches would assert themselves in this area, using the Constitution as their support in doing so. As James Madison once said, "Nothing has yet been offered to invalidate the doctrine that the meaning of the Constitution may as well be ascertained by the Legislative as by the Judicial authority." This is a quote not only for his time, but for ours as well.*

<u>Holding Justices to Their Oaths</u>
The problem with too many of the justices sitting on America's federal courts is that they exercise their judicial authority to make new law by ruling rights into and out of existence that are nowhere written in the plain text of the law. Perhaps the most famous instance of jurists of the Supreme Court breaking the Oath of Office occurred in the Supreme Court's ruling with regard to *Roe v. Wade*. It is obvious to everyone who has read the US Constitution that nowhere within the text of the Instrument is the issue of women's reproductive rights addressed or even implied. This does not mean abortion has to be illegal, but it does mean that it is up to the states to determine for themselves the legality of abortion and what the guidelines might be for obtaining one. If *Roe v. Wade* were overturned by a Constitutionalist Supreme Court, it would not be the end of abortions in America, but it would be a victory for the Tenth Amendment and a

vindication of every individual's right to control how the rules are written for such laws at a level of government closer to the people and easier for individuals to influence. It is high time that every federal jurist be held to his Oath of Office.

<u>Should Justices Who Rule Against the Laws as Written Be Impeached?</u>
Judges of the federal judiciary, who have made extra-legal or anti-Constitutional rulings, should be relieved of office, since they are not serving in "good behavior." Indeed, their bad behavior might be described, in Constitutional language, as misdemeanors. In Article III, Section 1, of the US Constitution, the following is stated: "The Judges, both of the supreme and inferior Courts, shall hold their Offices during good Behaviour, and shall, at stated Times, receive for their Services a Compensation, which shall not be diminished during their Continuance in Office." So, because good behavior is required, there is no real guarantee of lifetime service.

Furthermore, the Constitution, in Article II, Section 4, states the following: "The President, Vice President and all civil Officers of the United States, shall be removed from Office on Impeachment for, and Conviction of, Treason, Bribery, or other high Crimes and Misdemeanors." Misdemeanors would encompass such acts as legislating from the bench in contradiction to the law of the land and the US Constitution. In fact, Judge John Pickering, of the federal district court in New Hampshire, was impeached and removed from office for public drunkenness, among other wrongdoings that were probably impacted by his state of intoxication.

There were a total of four articles of impeachment for Pickering. Here are actual words from the fourth article: "That whereas for the due, faithful, and impartial administration of justice, temperance and sobriety are essential qualities in the character of a judge, yet the said John Pickering, being a man of loose morals and intemperate habits, on the 11th and 12th days of November, in the year 1802, being then judge of the district court in and for the district of New Hampshire, did appear on the bench of the said court for the administration of justice in a state of total intoxication, produced by the free and intemperate use of intoxicating liquors; and did then and there frequently, in a most profane and indecent manner, invoke the name of the Supreme Being, to the evil example of all the good citizens of the United States; and was then and there guilty of other high misdemeanors, disgraceful to his own character as a judge and degrading to the honor of the United States."

The case could be made that Pickering's misdemeanors were lesser offenses than the wholesale usurpation of the legislative powers of Congress. Thus, a justice of any court who legislates from the bench, so to speak, may be judged guilty of the far worse sin of usurping the prerogatives of the legislative branch, in contradiction to the Oath of Office in which a justice must swear, upon assuming office, to uphold the Constitution of the United States.

____

*For more on the issue of Constitutional Supremacy versus Judicial Supremacy, see Appendix C.

Article IV

"A people . . . possessed of the spirit of commerce, who see and who will pursue their advantages, may achieve almost anything." —George Washington

<u>Cooperation Among the Sovereign States</u>
Article IV of the United States Constitution outlines the duties states have to each other. It also provides for federal oversight of the following: 1) the admission of new states; 2) the changing of state boundaries; 3) that states admitted to the union will be guaranteed to have a republican form of government; and 4) that the federal government will protect any state from the invasion of its borders.

Among the duties that states have to each other, the Supreme Court has held that they include the following: 1) that public acts and proceedings in one state must be respected by all the others; 2) that one state may not discriminate against citizens of other states in favor of its own citizens when it comes to the protection of life, liberty, or property; 3) that any citizen has the right to travel through any other state for trade or other peaceful purposes; 4) that the benefits of a *Writ of Habeas Corpus* applies across states; and 5) that citizens from out of state hold the right to file court actions in any state in which they might find themselves, as well as the right to own personal or real property and the right to be taxed the same as other citizens within the state.

<u>The Fugitives from Labour Clause</u>
Article IV, Section 2, Clause Three, of the Constitution, known as the Fugitives from Labour Clause, compelled the return of escaped convicts by one state to another. Close reading of the language of this clause, however, will reveal why it came to be called the Fugitive Slave Clause, in instances when it was used to compel the return of runaway slaves. The clause reads as follows: "No person *held to service or labour in one state, under the laws thereof,* escaping into another, shall, in consequence of any law or regulation therein, be discharged from such service or labour, but shall be delivered up on claim of the party to whom such service or labour may be due." According to the language of the clause, it might apply to escaped convicts sentenced to hard labor, to indentured servants or apprentices, and to chattel slaves as well. The use of the phrase "under the laws thereof" to modify the words "labor in one state," make it clear that state laws control what constitutes legal servitude, not federal law; for there could be no allowance in the federal Constitution that slavery might be seen as being endorsed by the federal government. Since slavery is not mentioned directly in the clause, the Fugitive Slave Act of 1793 (and later the stricter Fugitive Slave Act of 1850—called the Bloodhound Law by abolitionists—which was a part of the Compromise of 1850) had to be enacted to allow the formal use of the Fugitives from Labour Clause for the return of chattel slaves.

The passage of the Thirteenth Amendment, banning slavery in the United States, is worded the way it is due to the existence of the Fugitives from Labour Clause: "Neither slavery nor involuntary servitude, *except as a punishment for crime whereof the party shall have been duly convicted,* shall exist within the United States, or any place subject to their jurisdiction." This wording limits the Fugitives from Labour Clause in its application to affecting only convicted felons and no one else. No longer shall the clause be utilized in practice as a Fugitive Slave Clause. Slave states may not, under the wording chosen for the Thirteenth Amendment, merely change their laws so special categories of labor might exist that would allow slavery to remain in existence, while simply being called something else.

<u>Republican Government Must Be Guaranteed</u>
Article IV, Section 4, Clause One, of the Constitution guarantees a republican form of government to every state entering the Union: "The United States shall guarantee to every State in this Union a Republican Form of Government." Since Article VII, the last article of the Constitution, stipulates that the Constitution must obtain the consent of the people in nine states out of thirteen before it takes effect in the ratifying states, a strong hint is given as to the how republican principles are meant to function. While requiring supermajorities to amend the Constitution, in order to protect the minority, unanimous consent is not required, lest the majority be held hostage by the minority, as was the case under the Articles of Confederation, which required the unanimous consent of all states before laws could be enacted or changed. This means that a republic balances the protection of the minority, no matter how small, with the right of the majority to have its way, if the majority be large enough.

<u>Protection From Invasion</u>
Article IV, Section 4, continues, stating in Clause Two that the United States "shall protect each of them [states] against Invasion; and on Application of the Legislature, or of the Executive (when the Legislature cannot be convened), against domestic Violence." This clause makes an open-borders policy of any kind illegal. Allowing unvetted illegal aliens into the country in large numbers constitutes a failure by the federal government to protect the states from invasion, especially when sizable numbers of people are entering the country and literally taking over parts of it, establishing entire areas that become criminal sanctuaries under the protection of corrupt political officials. (This kind of situation underscores the need for the right to keep and bear arms to be protected.) When such people are allowed to vote, in order to support the corrupt officials protecting them, they do so at the cost of depriving the citizenry of its legitimate voice—of its ability to elect uncorrupted officials to office who will protect the public. The problem arises that such a large-scale take-over by illegal aliens deprives citizens of the ability to enjoy a republican form of government, wherein they get to enjoy the privileges of citizenship. Instead, the invaders of the state find themselves enjoying privileges that no citizen enjoys, due to the power of the ballot box to deliver the illegal-alien population special privileges.

<u>Article IV Should Protect Americans From Losing Their Lives & Their Liberties</u>
A sad example of what can happen when the Constitution is not enforced—by allowing open-borders invasion by illegal migrants and by failing to guarantee a republican form of government—is the case of Jose Zarate from California: Although Zarate admitted that his gun discharged the shot that ricocheted and killed Kate Steinle, and despite the fact that he had seven prior felony convictions, Zarate was acquitted of murder charges and walked free, because he was a five-times-deported illegal alien and, therefore, a member of a protected criminal class in

28

the "sanctuary state" of California, a state that gives special privileges and protections to non-citizen criminals who are illegally in the United States. A US citizen would have been sent to prison for killing Steinle.

While many illegal aliens cause little or no harm to other Americans, the fact that illegal aliens are an unvetted cohort means that violent criminals are regarded on an equal footing with peaceful laborers, which is why illegal aliens ended up representing 36.7% of federal sentences in Fiscal Year 2014: 16.8% of federal drug-trafficking convictions, 20.0% of kidnaping/hostage-taking convictions, 74.1% of drug-possession convictions, 12.3% of money-laundering convictions, and 12.0% of murder convictions.

<u>America Is Supposed To Be a Nation of Legal, Not Illegal, Immigrants</u>
The United States of America is indeed a nation of immigrants; however, for the protection of all citizens, America must be a nation of *legal* immigrants. Constitutional originalists are *not anti-immigration*; they are *anti-illegal immigration*. There is a difference. Legal immigration law requires that immigrants be vetted for criminal history and checked for medical issues that might expose Americans to harm. Illegal immigration, when allowed or encouraged, causes the percentage of criminals in the general population to rise significantly, as well as costing peaceful, law-abiding citizens their lives in many instances. So, the difference between the two classes of immigrants—legal and illegal—is that legal immigrants are by and large safe, while, with illegal immigrants, the game being played is one of Russian Roulette. An important lesson, with regard to Article IV, Section 4, is that, without enforcement of Clause Two, protecting the states against invasion, it becomes much harder to guarantee Clause One, which gives to all citizens the right to a republican government, rather than a government hijacked by the voices of non-citizens and the illicit casting of their ballots.

The main advantage of Article IV, when it is enforced, is that it allows the American people peaceably to pursue trade and commerce within and without the borders of their own states. The federal government guarantees the integrity and the security of all the states.

Article V

"If in the opinion of the People the distribution or modification of the Constitutional powers be in any particular wrong, let it be corrected by an amendment in the way which the Constitution designates. But let there be no change by usurpation; for though this, in one instance, may be the instrument of good, it is the customary weapon by which free governments are destroyed. The precedent must always greatly overbalance in permanent evil any partial or transient benefit which the use can at any time yield." —George Washington

<u>Changing the Constitution</u>
Article V of the Constitution is all about the amendment process. The means of amending the Constitution is as follows: Two-thirds of the each chamber of Congress shall agree to alter the Constitution in some way—or else two-thirds of the state legislatures shall vote for a national Constitutional convention to propose any necessary change. Then any suggested change shall go before the American people, a majority vote of the legislatures of three-fourths of the states being necessary to the final adoption of any Constitutional amendment, or, alternatively, a vote of three-fourths of special ratifying conventions to be held in each state.

The signature of the president is not necessary to the adoption of a Constitutional amendment. The two-thirds vote to approve a law over any potential veto of a president is already a built-in feature of the amendment process. In 1798, the Supreme Court held that it is not necessary to place Constitutional amendments before the president for signature by this same logic.

It is also interesting to note that the Constitution does not require any timeline for the adoption of a Constitutional amendment. In fact, the Twenty-Seventh Amendment was proposed for passage in 1789, as a part of the original Bill of Rights. It was two centuries, however, before it was ratified, in 1992, by the vote of Michigan. (The Twenty-Seventh Amendment is a law requiring that no change in pay for senators and representatives shall occur until after one election of representatives shall have taken place.)

Articles VI & VII

"Hold on, my friends, to the Constitution and to the Republic for which it stands. Miracles do not cluster, and what has happened once in 6000 years, may not happen again. Hold on to the Constitution, for if the American Constitution should fail, there will be anarchy throughout the world." —Daniel Webster

Only the Ratified Constitution Is the Supreme Law of the Land

Article VI simply states that the Constitution of the United States is the supreme law of the land for all states ratifying the Constitution. All laws made under the authority of the Constitution will be binding on all states, and all treaties made and legally adopted under the Constitution shall likewise be binding on all states. State officials of every state will take an oath supporting the Constitution. And no religious test shall be required to hold any federal office.

The main importance of Article VI is in affirming that state courts must decide issues based primarily upon the United States Constitution and secondarily upon their own state constitutions. States are decidedly not allowed to make laws that come into conflict with the United States Constitution.

Article VII states that, once nine states have ratified the Constitution, the Constitution will begin to take effect among those states that have approved it. Article VII makes it clear that the new Constitution will only be binding on states that have ratified it.

Clarification Regarding Religious Tests

The stipulation that no religious test shall be required to hold office applies only to the federal government and only to office holders. This requirement that there be no religious test is not about anything else, other than holding office. It has been stated in several media sources that immigrants may not be held to any religious test, but this is not true. The Constitution does not bar religious tests for immigrants. Whether or not the people wish to impose any is another matter, but it is not un-Constitutional to vet immigrants for radical, dangerous, or terroristic religious practices.

The Danger of Making a Bad Treaty

The Supremacy Clause of the Constitution says, "This Constitution, and the Laws of the United States which shall be made in Pursuance thereof; *and all Treaties made, or which shall be made, under the Authority of the United States*, shall be the supreme Law of the Land; and the Judges in every State shall be bound thereby, any Thing in the Constitution or Laws of any State to the Contrary notwithstanding." This means that 100% transparency is important in the presentation of treaties made with other countries, since any treaty legally ratified by the US Senate will become the "supreme law of the Land; and the Judges in every State shall be bound thereby." This is why the presentation of the Trans-Pacific Partnership (TPP) treaty was so egregiously offensive in its secrecy. Even members of Congress were not allowed to have copies of this treaty, of which one of the signatories was Brunei, a Muslim country likely to require Sharia-compliant finance rules to be implemented in all banking and economic provisions of such a trade treaty. President Obama would only permit members of Congress to look at the treaty in a secret room from which no one was allowed to remove any of the information. There was therefore little transparency with the Congress and no transparency at all with the people.

<u>Would Admitting Part of the Sharia Into the US Constitution Imply Recognition of the Whole?</u>
The problem with allowing Sharia finance law to be ratified as part of a US treaty is that it would make portions of Islamic Sharia Law part of the US Constitution. It would not be too far afield for a lawyer to eventually argue that, since part of the Sharia has been accepted as the law of the land, that this would imply acceptance of Islamic law in its entirety. The problem with accepting the Sharia is that freedom is prohibited under Muslim law, lest Muhammad be criticized against the blasphemy rules that the Sharia insists be adhered to by all people, including non-Muslims. (The Sharia claims that all people come under its jurisdiction, not just Muslims.) Such rules becoming part of the US Constitution, due to a bad treaty's incorporation of the Sharia into the Constitution, would modify the First Amendment to outlaw any speech considered by Sharia Law to be blasphemy or hate speech, in accordance with Islamic law. There would, in essence, be no more free speech in America, since all speech would have to be Sharia-compliant. Other rights could be compromised as well, with Sharia-compliance being an absolute requirement.

<u>Jettisoning a Trojan Horse</u>
One of the least appreciated acts of President Donald Trump, in proportion to its high level of importance, has been the president's jettisoning of the Trojan Horse known as the TPP treaty. Besides the problems with admitting the Sharia into the Constitution, the TPP would have set up international tribunals to resolve trade disputes that would have proven to be quite complex and would have allowed other representatives from other countries to decide on trade rules that would impact US law by virtue of their having been written under the authority of a treaty passed by the US Senate. A web of administrative laws would likely ensue, about which the American people would have no say-so. These would be rules that Americans would have to live with, knowing that they were not even written by American bureaucrats, let alone the elected representatives of the American people. It is important for the people to know the Constitution, lest tricky politicians, who are experts in Constitutional manipulation, use their knowledge for malevolent purposes, and get away with it. There may well be future Trojan Horses to come, and the people and their representatives need to be capable of recognizing them as such.

The Bill of Rights

"It is now no more that toleration is spoken of as if it were the indulgence of one class of people that another enjoyed the exercise of their inherent Natural Rights, for happily, the Government of the United States, which gives to bigotry no sanction, to persecution no assistance, requires only that they who live under its protection should demean themselves as good citizens in giving it on all occasions their effectual support." —George Washington

<u>The Natural Rights That the People Insisted on Being *Writ Large*</u>
When the Bill of Rights was written, many thought it unnecessary to enshrine what they saw as Natural Rights in the Constitution. Others claimed that, since the states already guaranteed Natural Rights in their own constitutions, there was no need to enshrine those rights in a legal document for the country at large. Still others thought that choosing certain rights to put into a Bill of Rights would disqualify other Natural Rights as deserving of protection. There were also those who believed it would pose a danger to future Americans to codify these rights at the national level, since the national government might then find ways to use the letter of the law to twist the meanings intended in the Bill of Rights away from the original intents and purposes behind those meanings. However, by the same token, there were also patriots who did not trust government to protect the Natural Rights of citizens in absence of a written guarantee.

In the end, Americans decided on ten amendments to the Constitution, with simple, broadly worded language. The principles described are specific and direct, but also easily adaptable to various social contexts across time or distance. Personal policy preferences should not be considered when Constitutional interpretation comes into play. When there is any doubt as to what the people were thinking when they approved the original Constitutional language, writings from the time of its inception should be consulted. Many documents, articles, and letters are available for just such purposes, not the least of these being the Federalist and the Anti-Federalist papers. Jurists are to *read out of* the Constitution what was put there by those who argued for it and got it approved. They are not to *read into* the Constitution what they desire or what they think modern-day opinion polling might support.

What each American desires personally, or what polls well with the public, might change over time, but the Constitution remains steadfast in order to give America a consistency and predictability that will guide citizens in the planning of their day-to-day activities. Americans need to know it is safe to proceed with their daily business, without fear of sudden changes that could capriciously alter the legalities of their plans and actions. So when is it okay to change something in the Constitution? The Constitution itself says a change can be made when three quarters of the States decide a change is justified or needed. This is a safe enough consensus, and it has worked well to promote consistency and fairness in the long run.

The Constitution is intended to impose limits on federal policy-makers, making it difficult to impose their own beliefs on the American people, either through naked executive or legislative *fiat* or raw judicial power. Compared to the anti-Constitutional approach of those who call for the Constitution to be a "living document" whose meaning passively morphs over time, per the political whims of politicians and the factions to which they adhere, Constitutional conservatism holds that the meaning of what is written does not change, but holds, until a super-majority of the states actively decides that it should be altered through the amendment process, an approach that is not only reasonable, but lacking in political arrogance as well.

The First Amendment

"Whoever would overthrow the liberty of a nation must begin by subduing the freeness of speech." —Benjamin Franklin

"What is freedom of expression? Without the freedom to offend, it ceases to exist."
—Salman Rushdie

<u>Freedom of Expression, According to One's Conscience</u>
Amendment I to the Constitution guarantees that Congress shall make no law to abridge any of the following rights: 1) the freedom of religious expression; 2) the freedom of speech; 3) the freedom of the press; 4) the freedom of peaceable assembly; and 5) the freedom to petition the government to right wrongs.

The First Amendment is, at its root, a protection of one's emotional and intellectual property rights, maintaining one's Natural Right to worship God, to express one's ideas, and to publish one's views. The freedom to associate with anybody with whom one might wish to exchange views is also protected; for, just as tangible property may be exchanged, so may the products of one's intellect. Any violation of these Natural Rights is a crime against property. Even the right to petition the government is, in the end, a right to attempt a defense of one's property rights. The stealing of one's Natural Right to express ideas and feelings, by government force, is a tyrannical infringement of the people's freedom to trade intellectual property freely in the marketplace of ideas.

The First Amendment continues to protect Americans' Natural Rights to this day. Although both citizen and government groups have attempted, over time, to limit or cancel certain of these rights, there has been a First Amendment to come to the aid of Americans throughout the history of the American republic, thanks to the Founding Fathers.

There is little doubt that patriots feared that, without spelling out the right to religious freedom, there was a risk that the government could decide to prefer one religious sect over all the others, the way England had done; however, this time there would be no place to go to get away from the religious oppression allowed by a tyrannical state. Thus, the establishment of religious freedom was of foremost concern in the minds of America's Founders.

<u>Freedom of Religion Means Freedom of Expression Must Also Be Allowed</u>
Of course, if religious freedom were to be allowed, then speech must also be protected, lest those holding views in disfavor with the majority risk having their places of worship shuttered by the government. And, if religious literature of all varieties was to be allowed in print, freedom of the press would have to be guaranteed, lest the Bible itself one day risk being banned! Freedom of peaceable assembly would facilitate meetings of any and all groups that behaved nonviolently, not the least of which would be religious meetings by holders of divergent religious views. The right to petition the government to right wrongs, when it failed in protecting the aforementioned rights, was also important. So, there is a logical reason why the five rights enshrined by the First Amendment are all listed together.

<u>The Genesis of Free Speech & Press</u>
The formal genesis of free speech and press rights in America occurred in the 1730s when John Peter Zenger, an independent publisher of New York, gave voice to his criticism of the newly-appointed Governor William Cosby, who, upon his arrival in New York City, had replaced the chief justice of the colonial supreme court with a jurist more to his liking. Eventually, Zenger found himself charged with libel, due to his defamatory opinions of the governor, although those opinions were based upon factual information that Zenger thought he should be free to report. The case became a *cause célèbre* among the colonists, most of whom disapproved of the new governor's strong-arm tactics. Although Governor Cosby's appointed judge was in favor of Zenger's conviction, Zenger's political position eventually prevailed when his defender, Andrew Hamilton, decided to argue for jury nullification of the royal statute vexing his client; to this end, Hamilton advocated directly to members of the jury that circumstances called for the jury to nullify the law by a finding of "not guilty." After the closing arguments, the jury did, indeed, return just such a verdict.

Thus, it was a case of jury nullification that laid down the early expectation for free speech and free press in the minds of the American colonists, putting into play the notion that truth is a legitimate defense for defamatory expression. And, prior to Zenger's court case, it was actually Cato's "Reflections Upon Libelling," as published in one of Zenger's issues of *The New York Weekly Journal* that prefigured the legal argument Andrew Hamilton would eventually advance in defense of his client—the argument that "states have suffered or perished for not having, or for neglecting, the power to accuse great men who were criminals." (Cato was a *nom-de-plume* of British writers John Trenchard and Thomas Gordon.)

<u>A Restraint Upon Government</u>
The point needs to be made that the First Amendment is a restraint upon government, not upon private individuals or entities. Government is not allowed to give citizens criminal consequences for speaking their minds freely or for publishing their unexpurgated views. Government is not allowed to jail people for attending the meetings of particular groups or for expressing their individual religious beliefs. Government is also not allowed to imprison people who write letters to government offices to air their criticisms and concerns—something which is commonplace under socialist regimes. Also, government plays no role in determining what "hate speech" is or is not, since government might misuse such discretion to determine that minority views or anti-government dissent falls under that category.

<u>A One-Way Wall of Separation</u>
At Calvary Chapel, in Santa Ana, California, on Saturday, May 2nd, 2015, Pastor Rafael Cruz gave a special lesson wherein he addressed the issue of Thomas Jefferson's "Wall-of-Separation Letter to the Danbury Baptists." Cruz pointed out that this letter contains a reference to a "wall of separation between church and state" which has become famously misapplied, ever since Supreme Court Justice Hugo Black's twisting of its meaning beyond the limits of its original context, in the 1947 case *Everson v. Board of Education.*

Black's malappropriation of Jefferson's "wall-of-separation" metaphor has, unfortunately, become much-used shorthand for referring to the Establishment Clause of the First Amendment, while, in all actuality, the clause is there solely for the purpose of restraining the federal government from infringing the right of "We the People," and not for empowering such infringement to take place.

The Establishment Clause reads as follows: "Congress shall make no law respecting an establishment of religion, or prohibiting the free exercise thereof. . . ." Anyone can see that only the government is restrained by this clause. Justice Black, however, seems to have preferred the epistolary "wall-of-separation" metaphor to the Constitution's legal clause, because it could be easily repurposed to impose his own two-way concept of restraint that would include the requirement that religious people be likewise restrained in their religious expression—potentially shutting down much in the way of free religious expression by giving government the power to restrain the people, rather than the other way around, as the Framers originally intended.

As Pastor Rafael Cruz would have it, the time has come for patriots to re-establish Jefferson's original idea of a "one-way wall." But this will not likely occur, unless religious people decide not to be intimidated into "political correctness," which is nothing more than an idea whose goal is to promote self-censorship in favor of prescribed linguistic norms that straightjacket thought and kill diversity in the marketplace of ideas.

Although enforcing a regime of "political correctness" is anti-Constitutional and disallowed when it comes to the government's role, it is allowed by the people in the private sphere. Individuals are allowed to advocate for political correctness, if they choose to do so, and are allowed to self-censor, if that be their choice. But the government is not permitted by the Constitution to force the issue. Government promotion or censorship of any kind of speech is strictly forbidden. In fact, the government should not be in the business of funding any publishing, broadcasting, or content-providing companies, since doing so may politically encourage some forms of expression while deterring others; nor should government fund the creation of artwork of any kind, for the same reason.

<u>Rules for Civility in the Private Arena</u>
So, are there any instances where limiting an individual's freedom of expression is legally permitted? The answer to this question is yes; in the private sector, companies are allowed to enforce codes of verbal, written, and behavioral expression. Disrespecting the Stars and Stripes during the playing of the National Anthem is indeed punishable by the National Football League, which actually does have a policy on the books that standing for the Anthem is required. The NFL is a private business that must take into consideration what may or may not prove offensive to its customers and, as such, it is not subject to the Constitutional restraints placed upon a government entity.

Even government employers, such as public schools, are allowed to create speech codes which prohibit cursing or otherwise offensive forms of expression that might alienate students, parents, or coworkers. School district employees could be fired, in extreme cases, for offensive behavior. What is Constitutionally-restrained is criminal punishment by the government for exercising freedom of expression, not the enforcement of speech codes for employees written for the purpose of facilitating healthy interactions with members of the public.

Conscience in Religious Life
Under the First Amendment, religious freedom is allowed in daily life. This means that a rabbi or priest has the right to refuse to marry a gay couple. Rabbis and priests are individuals who are free to act in accordance with their religious beliefs, as are all Americans.

A gay couple has the right to get married, in line with the laws of the state in which the couple resides, but that same gay couple does not have the right, according to the original intent of the Constitution, to force a fellow human being into behaving in a way that is against his conscience. Finding another person to do the ceremony is the remedy that is permitted, according to the freedom-of-expression guarantees written into the First Amendment of the Constitution. Government force always comes with the threat of a person's being compelled at gunpoint into doing something by coercion, canceling the Natural Right to choose one's religious expression.

The Founders saw government as a necessary evil that had to be strictly limited in favor of promoting the non-coercive activities inherent in a civil society. There had to be a compelling reason for making a rule that would, under normal circumstances, be better left to the people to decide informally among themselves. Once formally created by government, rules become difficult to dispense with when no longer needed, while, when left to the people, rules are easily created, altered, canceled, or reinstated as needed. Rules for speech, as well as for other forms of expression, are no exception to this principle and remain within the province of civil society.

Conscience in Commerce
There are many reasons businesses turn down jobs. Sometimes, they are too busy to take on more work. At other times, they just do not have anyone available with the skills required for carrying out the job in question. But, from time to time, it is also possible that the business owner holds a conscientious objection to the job at hand. Anyone who is turned down by a vendor, for any reason at all, is free to patronize another vendor. That is the remedy one must seek in a free republic.

It is unfortunate, but true, that freedom is not free; it comes with the price of eternal vigilance and a willingness to expend one's efforts to defend freedom by any and all means necessary to ensure its continuance. The writing of this book, in an effort to advocate for Constitutionally-limited government and the Natural Rights protected by the US Constitution, is one example.

Free Speech & Civil Society: The Principle of Epistemic Humility
Also, in the defense of freedom, it is important to teach epistemic humility to American students. The word *episteme* (pronounced "eh-piss-tay-may") means "intellectually certain knowledge." To be true Americans, people must practice tolerance and willingly bestow freedom upon others

by allowing their differing ideas to be heard. Individuals must admit that they do not know everything and can benefit from hearing a different point of view. This is called "epistemic humility," and it is one of the nicer characteristics about freedom-loving Americans.

President Ronald Reagan was correct in his assessment that "Freedom is never more than one generation away from extinction." What America is in danger of losing—if Reagan's famous warning is not heeded, and the learning and sharing of America's tradition of freedom is not passed down from one generation to the next—is its tradition of prizing the toleration of differences. Students must be taught to listen to, and even appreciate, viewpoints which may differ with their own, even if some views create cognitive dissonance in their minds, for, without the understanding and valuing of differences, there can be little creativity or diversity of thought that will prove to be of benefit to society.

<u>The Threat Posed by Educational Indoctrination & the Ethic of Self-Censorship</u>
Academia today has become an over-credentialed engine of indoctrination. If the socialist, anti-Constitutional views being espoused by so many college professors these days are left unchallenged, the First Amendment is in real danger. Ray Bradbury, the author of *Fahrenheit 451*, once asserted that his job as a writer was "not to create the future, but to prevent it." The author of this book once asked Mr. Bradbury if he thought there could ever be book-burning in America. Mr. Bradbury responded by saying, "There is no need to burn any books. If you want to prevent people from learning what's in the books, you just have to get people to stop reading them." The follow-up comment was made that, on numerous occasions, fellow teachers, upon being asked if they had seen a particular report on *Fox News*, would reply that they would *never* deign to watch *Fox News*! "Well, there you have it, then," remarked Mr. Bradbury, "That's what I'm talking about. Self-censorship."

This disheartening willingness of so many Americans these days to self-censor puts a chilling effect into play, rendering entire areas of discussion off-limits. This is dangerous to freedom, because closed minds that are intentionally unaware of alternative ways of thinking and problem-solving are no better than willing slaves to the anti-freedom narrative; such people are of the variety which forms the very foundation of a socialist slave state.

<u>"My Mind's Made Up, Don't Confuse Me with the Facts!"</u>
Constitutional conservatives tend to read divergent ideas and consider a variety of viewpoints, finding this valuable in being able to understand different ways of thinking. (In this attempt to learn broadly, by considering different viewpoints—what is known as a "liberal education"—the advocates of Natural Rights are seeking to conserve the classical liberalism embedded in the Constitution by the Founders, who believed in empowering the individual by limiting the coercive capabilities of the government.) Constitutionalists believe that problems should be solved with the most freedom possible; that people should try to problem-solve among themselves first, based upon valid factual information and an understanding of the historical successes and failures of various approaches, before bringing the authorities into the mix; and that state intervention should be put off as long as possible, in an effort maintain flexibility in

problem-solving. The unwillingness of so many to participate in a civil-society tradition—one that puts people first and government last—only exacerbates problems. To lovers of limited government, those who oppose free speech appear eager to live with state-directed prescriptions, rather than working things out with others—putting government first and people last.

Constitutionalists who love individual freedom tend to place more trust in the notion of giving power to the people, while maintaining a healthy distrust in the political power wielded by power-greedy government actors. In order to work well with others to solve problems together, an understanding of how different people think is essential. It is the culture of individual freedom that promotes this principle of seeking first to understand others, before trying to communicate or problem-solve with them, whereas, in a culture of government force, understanding the Other is of no great import, since what the Self wants is a political connection in order to bring about the situation desired by use of government *fiat*. To live as a free human being, with one's Natural Rights intact, free speech is an absolutely vital ingredient, lest all safeguards for individual freedom and mutual understanding be lost*.

<u>How the Desire Never to Be Offended Endangers Freedom</u>
A world of increasing physical and emotional comfort poses a threat to the tradition of free speech. The desire for physical comfort—and the instant respite from pain modern medications bring—has led many to demand emotional comfort as well. Some people are insisting that there be maintained, anywhere and everywhere, a "right" not to feel offended. This imagined right to a guarantee of good feeling is untenable in a pluralistic society. The only way to rid civil society of its tradition of pluralism would be by government force, which is contrary to the entire notion of a civil society. Also, everyone's holding the same shade of opinion is far from desirable, since this would leave people uninformed on many levels and vulnerable to being blindsided by events that could not have been imagined or foreseen within the narrow confines of a biased, state-approved ideology.

<u>Marching Nazis, in Skokie, Illinois</u>
In 1977, approximately thirty members of the National Socialist Party of America wanted to stage a march in Skokie, Illinois, wearing Nazi uniforms with swastika armbands and carrying a large, red banner that would also bear the swastika, in the historic style of Adolf Hitler's National Socialist German Workers Party. Skokie, at the time, had 70,000 inhabitants, 40,000 of whom were Jewish and 5,000 of whom were Holocaust survivors. Naturally, Skokie did not want such a demonstration, so a court order was sought to stop the event, based upon the fear that such a display would incite hatred against the Jews. Violence was also a feared response, given a community where feelings about the Holocaust ran high.

The American Civil Liberties Union took the case on behalf of the Nazis, arguing that the First Amendment protected the free speech of the Nazis who wanted to hold a march in a Jewish area. After the US Supreme Court ordered a full hearing before the Illinois Supreme Court, the Nazi group received the ruling it wanted: the march would go forward, as symbolic free speech protected by the US Constitution. The fact that such speech might promote feelings of racial or religious hatred did not matter. "Retaining meaning in civil rights," wrote the Illinois Supreme Court, "particularly those many of the founding fathers believed sufficiently important as to delay the approval of the Constitution until they could be included in the Bill of Rights, seldom seems to be accomplished by the easy cases, however, and it was not so here. . . . [O]ur Regret at the use appellees plan to make of their rights is not in any sense an Apology for upholding the First Amendment. The result we have reached is dictated by the fundamental proposition that if these civil rights are to remain vital for all, they must protect not only those [whom] society deems acceptable, but also those whose ideas it quite justifiably rejects and despises."

Louis Brandeis has famously written that "fear breeds repression; that repression breeds hate; that hate menaces stable government; that the path of safety lies in the opportunity to discuss freely supposed grievances and proposed remedies; and that the fitting remedy for evil counsels is good ones." In other words, more healthy speech—rather than the suppression of unhealthy speech—is the correct prescription necessary for true understanding and problem-solving.

<u>Burning the Flag</u>
Because true freedom means that even the most unpopular speech is protected, the Supreme Court has ruled, in *Texas v. Johnson*, that the burning of the United States flag is a protected form of expression under the First Amendment. This communicative act, considered by the Court to be symbolic speech, is an act generally frowned upon by self-described Constitutional conservatives. Yet this promotion of individual freedom is exactly the point of the Constitution in the first place, and Constitutionalists have applauded the Supreme Court's decision, even if doing so did not mean they would choose to act in the manner allowed by the decision.

Evelyn Beatrice Hall famously characterized the libertarian ideals of Voltaire by saying, "I disapprove with what you say, but I will defend to the death your right to say it." This kind of thinking was a tremendous influence on the Framers of the Constitution. And what the Constitution is really designed to do, in the end, is to prevent the disestablishment of freedom in favor of tyranny. It is about constraining the government from limiting any and all expressions of the people.

<u>Is Free Speech Permitted Only for *Some*, on an Internet Funded & Built by *All*?</u>
It has become obvious that social media, far from becoming enablers of free expression, have taken to the practice of discrimination against patriotic conservative or libertarian voices while giving succor to such unsavory notions as anti-Semitism and Holocaust denial. Their defense is that, as a private business, they are allowed to block whatever speech they wish, even if doing so intentionally discriminates against libertarians or conservatives. The problem with this defense when it comes to an Internet-based business model, however, is that social media depend on the Internet that the entire American people built. Yes, the Internet was developed and built using public money—taxpayer dollars supplied by *all* Americans of *all* political stripes and opinions.

So, Facebook, Twitter, and others are using taxpayer resources provided by *all* while only allowing free speech by *some*—the same kind of discrimination once practiced against blacks. Social media companies have now become home to the ideology of Jim Crow. The only difference is that political ideology is the new basis for discrimination, rather than skin color.

Until such time as social media build their own private equivalent of the Internet, they must adhere to the Constitution as they operate within the public square that the Internet represents. The prejudicial tyranny posed by tech-company elites is a very real challenge to liberty today, just as the bigoted injustice of the Jim Crow elites once posed a similar challenge. If socialist Nazi protestors were allowed to parade their hatred through Skokie, due to their Constitutional right to demonstrate anti-Semitic views in a *tangible* town square—which is the same kind of speech that Facebook now tolerates on its platform, in accordance with the First Amendment— then why do patriots who are philo-Semitic and freedom-loving not hold the same right to share their love of America or of Israel in a *virtual* town square (which is the Internet cyber-world upon whose ground social media operate)?

———

*See Appendix D for more on the topic of why free speech is vital to a free republic. Also, to learn more about the limits placed on free speech by colleges and universities, the writings of Greg Lukianoff are highly recommended: http://www.thefire.org/author/greglukianoff/.

The Second Amendment

"Among the natural rights of the Colonists are these: First, a right to life; Secondly, to liberty; Thirdly, to property; together with the right to support and defend them in the best manner they can. These are evident branches of, rather than deductions from, the duty of self-preservation, commonly called the first law of nature." —*Samuel Adams*

<u>The Right of the People to Keep & Bear Arms</u>
Amendment II to the Constitution guarantees "the right of the people" to arm themselves for self-defense. The Library of Congress records the amendment to be written and punctuated as follows—per Thomas Jefferson's authentication of the text in his role as Secretary of State: "A well regulated Militia being necessary to the security of a free State, the right of the people to keep and bear Arms shall not be infringed." When asked who the militia was, Founder George Mason answered, "They consist now of the whole people, except for a few public officers."

The right to protect one's person against harm is perhaps the most serious of property rights, and, as such, it must never be abridged or violated. Since a person's own human body is his most intimate personal property, which also functions as the very vehicle that carries his human life as precious cargo, depriving the individual of his Natural Right to keep and bear the same arms that any willing lawbreaker may find at his disposal ultimately risks depriving the individual of his most valuable possession—his life. Because guns are necessary to save innocent lives, any ban on their use by law-abiding citizens only works to allow criminals—who never feel obligated to obey such bans—to exercise a right of self-preservation that law-abiding citizens do not enjoy.

<u>The Capacity to Live Without Fear</u>
The right of the people to keep and bear arms harkens back to the English Bill of Rights of 1689, which guarantees the right of Protestants to have arms for their defense. It is armed defense that protects all the other rights, including the right to "life, liberty, and the pursuit of happiness" written into the Declaration of Independence, in 1776, by Thomas Jefferson. In a speech to the National Press Club, on September 11, 1997, Charlton Heston said, "[The Second Amendment] alone offers the absolute capacity to live without fear. The right to keep and bear arms is the one right that allows 'rights' to exist at all."

<u>Power to the People for the Defense of Innocent Life</u>
Giving power to the people meant granting Americans the right to bear arms, without reference to any specific type of weaponry. This has had the intended effect of giving the American people the right to defend themselves with the same weaponry that is at the disposal of their criminal adversaries. The right to defend innocent life was considered by America's Founders to be a Natural Right that could not be taken away, which is why the "right of the people" is so clearly written into the Second Amendment. Indeed, it is this "right of the people to keep and bear arms" that allows a "well regulated militia" to exist at all. The wording of the amendment is quite specific on this point of privileging the rights of the people over the power of the state. In fact, when men reported for training in their local militia units, in colonial America, they were

43

required to bring their own firearms, since an armed citizenry pre-existed any organized militia.

There have been many attempts by private, as well as government, entities to abridge or cancel the right to self-defense, at both national and state levels, regardless of the fact that areas of the country with higher rates of lawful gun ownership have lower rates of criminal gun murder. The Founders suspected that, eventually, the government would begin to prize the power to control people above doing what is good for the people's protection, which is why the amendment ends by saying, "shall not be infringed."

<u>Trusting People, Distrusting Government</u>
The Founding Fathers were, in fact, so suspicious of government power that they did not believe the national government should possess its own standing army. One must keep in mind the fact that the British government had once been their government; and one need only read a history lesson to know how the colonists' own government had turned on them with what could only be described as an unprecedented and unwarranted degree of martial oppression.

Because of the British Crown's heavy-handed despotism, the Founders had no choice but to learn the difference between how government actors behave versus private individuals and came to regard government as a necessary evil that required strict limits, for the sake of preserving liberty. Their distrust of state power was so serious that, although they granted the federal government the power to create a military force for temporary purposes, Article I, Section 8, acts as a constraint on its ability to raise and support a standing military. The federal government is allowed "[t]o raise and support Armies, but no Appropriation of Money to that Use shall be for a longer Term than two Years." This is why a National Defense Authorization Act must be passed every one or two years, to continue the existence and support of America's armed forces. The Founders placed their faith in an armed populace—in the people, not the government—so that that the people might be capable of defending America against invasion by outside forces, as well as against government tyranny perpetrated by "public officers" within its own borders. The "enemy within" was as serious a consideration as any foreign invader. It was not desirable, in the minds of the large majority of Americans, that this faith in, and empowerment of, the people should ever change; to this end, they wished a written guarantee of its permanence, which is why the Second Amendment was born.

<u>Arms Control Is People Control: Why the Right to Bear Arms Is America's First Freedom</u>
In American history, it must also be recalled that the actual government policy that rankled the colonists more than any other, and eventually sparked the beginning of Revolutionary War, was that of a public officer—General Thomas Gage, the acting governor of Massachusetts—whose policy was to regulate the firearms of the American colonists by confiscating civilian-owned guns and ammunition. What Gage knew—what all agents of government know—is that gun control is people control. When the victims are disarmed ahead of time, the government can treat the people however it chooses, without fear. Indeed, it is the people who must live in fear, not only of their own tyrannical police state but of run-of-the-mill criminals as well.

44

The situation continued to deteriorate until, on April 19, 1775, 700 Redcoats marched on Lexington and Concord to seize the weapons stored there. Paul Revere made his famous ride to warn the militias in the area, causing 200 men from 16 to 60 to meet to oppose the British at Lexington Green, while still others hid their weapons. Defeated at Lexington, the Americans struck back at Concord, defeating the British forces there. Later that same night, the Siege of Boston began, and the American Revolutionary War was underway. The Americans used an armed militia—regulated by the people themselves, of course—to defend their Natural Right to keep and bear arms, along with all their other God-given rights. The right to keep and bear arms is to this day considered by many to be America's First Freedom.

To quote Charlton Heston* from a speech he gave before the National Press Club, on September 11, 1997, "I say that the Second Amendment is, in order of importance, the first amendment. It is America's First Freedom, the one right that protects all the others. Among freedom of speech, of the press, of religion, of assembly, of redress of grievances, it is the first among equals. It alone offers the absolute capacity to live without fear. The right to keep and bear arms is the one right that allows 'rights' to exist at all. . . . [T]here is no such thing as a free nation where police and military are allowed the force of arms but individual citizens are not. That's a 'Big Brother knows best' theater of the absurd that has never boded well for the peasant class, the working class, or even for reporters."

<u>The Founders' Faith in Armed Defense of Innocent Life</u>
The Founders knew that weapons were essential for defending innocent life, so they put their faith in the fact that the presence of firearms in all areas of public life would deter criminals from carrying out as many evil deeds as they otherwise might, since their risks of being wounded or killed would rise dramatically in the absence of gun-free zones. This is in evidence in the town of Kennesaw, Georgia, where gun ownership is a legal requirement. Albeit the law is not strictly enforced, the statement it makes is strong enough to keep violent crime to profoundly low levels.

<u>The Second Amendment Is Needed Now More Than Ever</u>
It is alarming how many people have lost an appreciation of the importance of the Second Amendment. There are those who wish to disarm the American people, claiming that it would be safer for people to do without firearms. But such pretensions are the very height of foolishness. Can it really be believed that, if law-abiding persons were to lay down their arms, criminals would follow suit by giving up theirs as well? And do requirements for background checks and limits on magazine capacity actually cause criminal actors to shrink from purchasing guns or magazines on the black market or stealing them from law-abiding citizens? And what about the old adage that goes, "When seconds count, the police are only minutes away"? Indeed, it is rare that the police ever arrive in response to a 9-1-1 call in time to save victims of a home invasion from being sexually assaulted or needlessly murdered.

Thomas Jefferson once said, "The laws that forbid the carrying of arms . . . disarm only those who are neither inclined nor determined to commit crimes. . . . Such laws make things worse for the assaulted and better for the assailants; they serve rather to encourage than to prevent

homicides, for an unarmed man may be attacked with greater confidence than an armed man."
This is why the Founders wrote the Second Amendment without infringements. They knew that
an atmosphere of firearms everywhere, in the hands of the law-abiding, would be the best
deterrent to violence and murder. The Framers of the Constitution knew that, without a "right of
the people" to arm themselves, that "shall not be infringed," it would prove difficult indeed to
stop an ill-intentioned—or just plain ignorant—future government from ultimately relieving the
people of all their Natural Rights. The phrase "shall not be infringed" is a line in the sand drawn
by America's Founders, so that it is not only illegal to pass any law that interferes with the right
to self-defense, but it is also a violation of an office-holder's Oath of Office to do so. In an ideal
world, anyone who fails to enforce the Second Amendment, or any other right guaranteed by the
Constitution, should be turned out of office by the voters.

______

*See the full transcript of Charlton Heston's Speech at the National Press Club, in Appendix E.

The Third Amendment

"Here, sir, the people govern." —Alexander Hamilton

<u>Quartering Soldiers in People's Homes Is Not Permitted</u>
Amendment III to the Constitution bars the government from stationing soldiers in private homes, in a clear nod to property rights. It empowers the Congress to make a law prescribing how this might be done during wartime only, but the Congress has never taken up this issue; thus, it remains illegal for the government to station soldiers in private residences, even in times of war. (The courts have also ruled that apartment dwellers enjoy the same rights in living spaces leased from property owners.) Depriving people of the free use of their property without just compensation would be stealing, and the Third Amendment seems to acknowledge this.

The Third Amendment is important with regard to real property rights. It is an example of how independent Americans, by right, possess a great deal of freedom from government intrusion. While it is an almost-forgotten amendment of the Bill of Rights, it does remain important to this day as a practical safeguard against military, or paramilitary, government entities that would claim the use of private property for their own purposes, against the will of the property owner. The Third Amendment is the amendment to the Constitution that addresses the right to be in control of one's immediate living space. While the First Amendment addresses internal intellectual property rights, and the Second Amendment is concerned with the physical body as property of the individual, the Third Amendment moves outward into the realm of the living environment immediately surrounding one's human body. Its very existence means that the individual holds the right to live in one's own private abode, free of interference by the state, unless permission is given to enter. The strength of the statement this amendment makes for the rights of property owners cannot be denied. When it comes to a contest of rights between government agencies and private property owners, the rights of the people hold pre-eminence. People run the government, not the reverse. The government is accountable to the people, not the other way around. Not even the soldiers of the state may enter private property without permission. Thus, government exists to serve the people as an agency of the people. The people of a free republic are not subservient to the purposes of the state and, therefore, the principle of civilian control of the military is also affirmed by the Third Amendment.

The Mitchell family of Henderson, Nevada, filed suit against their local police on July 1, 2013, with regard to an incident that occurred on July 10, 2011. Allegedly, the police broke down the door of the Mitchell household and occupied their Henderson residence by force, after the Mitchells refused a request to allow police to be stationed in their home for neighborhood surveillance purposes. The police arrested Mr. Mitchell and consumed his family's food, water, and air-conditioning. The use of military-style tactics to occupy the house, as well as the way in which the police used the family's resources without permission, led to a Third Amendment claim being made against the city of Henderson, Nevada. The police eventually dropped all charges against the Mitchells, although the Mitchells persisted in their complaint against the police, who almost certainly classify as soldiers of the state, per the Third Amendment.*

---

*Read more about the Third Amendment in Appendix F.

The Fourth Amendment

"The natural liberty of man is to be free from any superior power on Earth, and not to be under the will or legislative authority of man, but only to have the law of nature for his rule."
—Samuel Adams

"The proper role of government is exactly what John Stuart Mill said in the middle of the 19th century in On Liberty. *The proper role of government is to prevent other people from harming an individual. Government, he said, never has any right to interfere with an individual for that individual's own good. The case for prohibiting drugs is exactly as strong and as weak as the case for prohibiting people from overeating. We all know that overeating causes more deaths than drugs do. If it's in principle okay for the government to say you must not consume drugs because they'll do you harm, why isn't it all right to say, 'You must not eat too much because you'll do harm'? Why isn't it all right to say, 'You must not try to go in for skydiving because you're likely to die'? Why isn't it all right to say, 'Oh, skiing, that's no good, that's a very dangerous sport, you'll hurt yourself'? Where do you draw the line?"* *—Milton Friedman*

<u>The Right to Be Left Alone</u>
Amendment IV of the Constitution reinforces the right of the people to be secure in their persons and places of residence, without fear of government intrusion, except in cases where authorities have probable cause to believe that illegal activities are occurring. In other words, this amendment protects an important property right, without which no right to privacy may be claimed. Suspicious activities must be observed directly by the police, or a search warrant issued upon probable cause, before authorities may search one's person or one's personal property. And the only areas of a residence allowed to be searched are those places that are specified in the search warrant. Also, the only objects the authorities may seize are those objects described in the search warrant; anything else, legal or illegal, must be left behind by the police.

The Fourth Amendment is a powerful ally to privacy advocates and an important limitation on government power. In theory, as long as a one does not harm anyone else—due to any effect of what one chooses to do behind closed doors—then one effectively maintains the right to continue doing whatever one pleases within the private precincts of one's own home. If there is no harm or perception of harm to any particular party—no infringement upon anyone else's rights or freedoms—then there is no foul and no penalty to be exacted. This is liberty.

To procure a warrant for a search of a person's private sphere—including one's person or private vehicle while outside one's residence, or one's emails or bank records—the government must receive a sworn statement by a witness that makes a judge believe something illegal has taken place or is taking place. All persons have a Natural Right to be left alone by the police power, unless there be evidence of some compelling need to invade that privacy for reasons owing to the public safety.

So, the Fourth Amendment moves outward yet again from the mere living space around the individual into the arena of public justifications for the invasion of that private sphere, which would include any activities harmful to the neighborhood or the community at large that might originate within the precincts of the property in question.

San Rafael's Smoking Ban
Communities in California, such as San Rafael, have passed laws banning the smoking of cigarettes inside one's own home, if the property shares a common wall with another property (such as in a condominium). This is a statute that clearly violates one's property rights. It may be legal to sell a property with a deed restriction against smoking that the buyer must accept upon purchase, but a naked ban of someone's property rights is problematic. The San Rafael statute does not even require that the smoke bother a person inhabiting the adjacent property, before the ban might be invoked. It is simply an outright ban against one's private addiction while living one's life upon one's own property. From a Constitutional standpoint, this poses serious concerns with regard to government intrusion into one's privacy.

Smoking regulations in common areas are legal, since there is a reasonable expectation that one be able to enjoy a smoke-free environment in the public arena, even with regard to adjoining rooms' shared ventilation within public buildings. California's ban on smoking in any non-private building or in any place of work has not led to serious challenges or complaints, since its being implemented in 1995, because no expectation of privacy or privacy rights (beyond the intellectual and physical integrity of one's own mind and body) exists in any community setting.

Warrantless Recordings
On July 22, 2016, Phyllis Hamilton, a federal judge, ruled that law enforcement may place recording devices in public places, since this does not violate the Fourth Amendment guarantee against warrantless searches and privacy protections. Four men were accused by law enforcement of conspiring to restrain competition by agreeing not to compete with each other during auctions for foreclosed properties. There was no invasion into anyone's private living space in order to obtain the recordings, according to the court ruling, even if the men claimed that they had been holding a private huddle that should be protected by the Fourth Amendment. Judge Hamilton's point was that the men's covert conversation occurred in an unprotected public space; had the men carried out their plan to restrain competition inside a private home, a surveillance recording executed by the police power would have been ruled inadmissible .

So, this begs the following question: What if microphones on the street are powerful enough to listen to private conversations taking place inside a house or apartment? It is a good question, the answer to which would be that such a recording constitutes an illegal search, unless a warrant has been issued allowing such a search, along the same lines of justification as a wiretap. And even then, such a warrant would have to specify, according to Constitutional guidelines, what information was to be sought—or listened for—and what kinds of utterances were allowed to be collected as evidence. Any other information found, with regard to off-topic matters, would have to be ruled inadmissible in a courtroom. The lesson is this: In public, there is implied consent to record any sounds or sights extant. It is only in one's own private living area that there is a clear-cut expectation of privacy that may be legally enforced.

<u>Flyovers</u>
There is very little case law applicable in the area of drone flyovers of a person's property. So, questions arising as to the enforcement of public nudity statutes on naked sunbathers who are exposing themselves in private, fenced-off areas of their own property are still an issue whose boundaries have not been fully tested. Or what if someone were to sell a controlled substance to another person in a private area of one's own grounds? Two Supreme Court cases, *California v. Ciraolo* and *Florida v. Riley*, held that flyover surveillance at 1,000 and 400 feet, respectively, did not violate the Fourth Amendment, although one justice, Sandra Day O'Connor, found that public use of altitudes lower than 400 feet was sufficiently rare as to constitute a violation of the reasonable expectation of privacy. These 1986 and 1989 cases impacting flyovers by small planes and helicopters observing and photographing people's behavior inside the confines of someone's private property are now dated and—in an age of drones—may be in need of further clarification. Drones almost always fly at very low altitudes, especially at or below 400 feet. And, with drone delivery of parcels and packages becoming a realistic option for commercial retailers, future cases of evidence collection—either on purpose or by accident—are almost assured to occur when, eventually, law enforcement ends up collecting and using such evidence in a court of law.

<u>Riley v. California</u>
The Supreme Court's decision, in *Riley v. California*, was important in its declaration that the contents of cell phones are both qualitatively and quantitatively different from other items found upon an individual's person, since the contemporary cell phone is no different than an extension of one's home computer in its storage capabilities and its ability to access bank accounts, email accounts, and a plethora of other private accounts and networks. In order to search a cell phone, according to the Court, a warrant must first be obtained, or else some case-specific circumstance invoked, that might allow an exception to a warrant under the banner of probable cause.

What is allowed by the Supreme Court's ruling is the seizure of the cell phone itself and the prevention of any act that might erase or alter data contained within the phone at the time of its seizure, since this would constitute the destruction of evidence while waiting for a warrant; this means the police may prevent the cell phone user from powering off the phone, removing its battery, or placing it inside a Faraday shield, bag, or cage. Of course, consent to search the contents of the cell phone would release authorities from the need to obtain a warrant.

<u>The Center of Discourse</u>
In any case, the center of discourse, when it comes to the Fourth Amendment, is around what people's reasonable claims might be with regard to privacy rights, rather than going from the assumption that the state can merely use any information it manages to collect in whatever way it pleases, which is what occurs in most foreign jurisdictions. This is an important right that is being put at risk nowadays, with the proliferation of cell phones bearing microphones and cameras, as well as computers and other high-tech devices capable of surveilling Americans in their own homes, almost all of which are linked to the Internet and therefore are exposed to the risk of hacking by government and its agents.

The Fifth Amendment

"Facts are stubborn things; and whatever may be our wishes, our inclination, or the dictates of our passions, they cannot alter the state of facts and evidence." —John Adams

Protections Against Property Confiscation

Amendment V of the Constitution provides several trial protections: 1) the right to be indicted by a grand jury before a felony charge can be tried in court; 2) the right to remain silent so as not to incriminate oneself; 3) the right to be tried only once for a crime (so as to avoid being put in "double-jeopardy"); 4) the right to Due Process (similar to the Fourteenth Amendment) and the Equal Protection that implies; and 5) the requirement that the exercise of eminent domain by the state be paired with fair compensation for the property the government has taken for public use.

The Right to Due Process guaranteed by this amendment reinforces the property right that one's person—a form of private property—is protected from unjust incarceration. Likewise disallowed is the unfair confiscation of one's real property, without fair compensation, which would unfairly harm the owner of any real property taken by the state. The seizure of property is fair only if it is for necessary public use and reimbursed at a fair market rate. If the property taken is given to another person or entity for purposes of private benefit, the crime of theft has occurred, since one person has been injured by the state for the benefit of another person or group of persons. This is wealth redistribution—a criminal act against one's property rights—rather than fair use.

The right under this amendment not to be tried twice for the same crime prohibits the state from repeated acts of bullying. If the facts of a case are strong enough to convict, then arguing the case a second time before a different jury should prove unnecessary. Also, given time, witnesses may become unavailable; some may emigrate or otherwise elope from the jurisdiction, while others may become ill or demented, and still others may die. All such circumstances could deprive a person of the right to a fair rehearing.

The Case of Amanda Knox

Amanda Knox, an American expatriate living in Italy, was accused of murder and served four years in prison before her conviction was overturned. After Knox's return to the United States, Italy decided to try her yet again, which constitutes a state of double-jeopardy that would be disallowed under the Constitution of the United States. The question is this: Does the US Constitution protect Ms. Knox from extradition back to Italy?

Although the Constitution's prohibition against double-jeopardy prosecutions does not extend to other countries, it is common for US extradition treaties to contain language protecting Americans against extradition when the person extradited might face double-jeopardy prosecution for the same crime. The wording of the extradition treaty between the United States and Italy, written during the Reagan era, applies to Ms. Knox, and its language contains provisions to protect Americans against the tyrannical practice of double-jeopardy prosecution.

So, Ms. Knox is safe from extradition and may proceed with her life plans.

<u>The Supreme Court Makes a Big Mistake: The Case of *Kelo v. the City of New London*</u>
Kelo v. the City of New London was an important case concerning eminent domain heard by the Supreme Court, because at issue was the question of whether or not a government could justify the taking of private property, under the Takings Clause of the Fifth Amendment, for the purpose of development by a private individual or entity, as long as that purpose coincided with the government purpose of higher tax collections that might result from such private development. In *Kelo*, a Connecticut statute allowing eminent domain for economic development was at issue. The finding of the Supreme Court in the case was actually wrong, since the plain language of the Constitution gives no exception in the Takings Clause for giving license to the government for the taking of real property for the purpose of increasing tax collections. Taking land for public *use* is not the same thing as taking land for the public *purpose* of increasing the land's taxable value to the government.

<u>Constitutional Expansion of Government Power Is Generally Illegitimate</u>
The danger of this decision lies in its justification of government confiscation of real property, if it be for the economic purpose of allowing developers to take possession of a valuable piece of land for the mutual benefit of the private land developer and the government tax collector. The Constitution is clearly opposed to this state of affairs. It is difficult to imagine a more abusive interpretation of the Takings Clause, since it would allow the government to make a simple declaration of intent to increase tax collections in order to permit a politically-connected developer to conspire with the taxing authority to steal someone else's hard-earned real estate. The decision constitutes a newly created government power that has never previously existed within the history of the republic. Rulings that create new government powers are extremely suspect, and, in almost every instance, should not lawfully occur in a federal court proceeding.

<u>A Lawyerly Mindset, Divorced From Concerns About the People's Liberty, Is Problematic</u>
Perhaps one of the problems with the Supreme Court is the fact that it has been left entirely to the lawyers to run the Court. (Actually, there is no clause in the Constitution that states any intention that only lawyers be allowed to sit upon the Supreme Court.) Lawyers love to use their minds to invent new meanings and to create and destroy lines of thinking which they either prefer or despise. When it comes to the Constitution, lawyers sitting as jurists upon the Court must make a good-faith effort to see issues from the perspective of empowering the people and limiting the state. The Constitution was not written for the purpose of giving the government more power, and it was not written to give lawyerly jurists a license to invent meanings out of the wording of the document that are not there already. The Constitution is the settled law of the land, and, as such, must only have meanings *read out of it* that have been put there by the representatives of the people; its purpose is not to have new meanings *read into it*, based upon unfounded theories of what people might want the document to mean today, especially if such meanings work to broaden—rather than limit—government power.

The first thing one should do when studying the original intent of a Constitutional clause, before one even cracks open a book or clicks open a website, is to pose some simple questions: 1) Does the clause in question limit the government in some way? If it is a restrictive clause, then its meaning should remain restrictive, in no way being reinterpreted to expand the government's power without a law or a Constitutional amendment being enacted. 2) If the clause actually defines a government power, then does the new theory about how that power might be construed simply make a logical leap forward, given a modern context, or is the new theory one which, more than providing an update in its application, actually makes the government more difficult for the people to rein in? For example, since the Congress is allowed to create post roads, as one of its Enumerated Powers, does that mean the Congress can allow the post office to run an email service as a way of creating a new way to deliver mail, as a logical leap forward into a domain of service for the post office that is not qualitatively different from its traditional role?

The People's Law in the People's Language
Perhaps the most famous lawyer joke of all time is from William Shakespeare's *Henry VI*, wherein Dick the Butcher, for the betterment of the country, makes this suggestion: "The first thing we do, let's kill all the lawyers." Dick's remark is not without a sense of humor, since humor is nothing more than an attempt to tell the truth about a problem in a way that is surprising, catching the audience off-guard and thus evoking the nervous reaction of laughter in response. What is no joking matter is when American lawyers claim to have sole possession of the correct legal faculties for interpretation of the US Constitution, since this is a false claim indeed.

The Constitution is the tool by which the people limit their government. The Constitution is written in the language of lay people and has actually elevated much in the way of plain language to the status of legal language, a good example of which is the very term "Takings Clause." Even the legal terminology embedded within the Constitution's text is mostly terms like *Habeas Corpus* and other common legal usages of the time when the document was written. Any terms that might not have been universally understood were soon absorbed by the public at large, during the time of public debate before the ratification of the Constitution. The point is that the language of the Constitution belongs to the people for the legitimate purpose of limiting government power, not to lawyers for the corrupt purpose of enlarging government power.

The Constitutional Is Teachable
The people are not only allowed to read and interpret the document without lawyerly help, they are actually encouraged to do so. If it were impossible for the people to understand the language of the Constitution, or if the people's law were not meant for public consumption and comprehension (a ridiculous proposition on the face of it), then the Constitution would never have become the subject of instruction in the public schools. Any legal meanings not apparent to members of the American citizenry at large are, therefore, difficult to justify and should not exist. This is why the idea of original intent is so important. What teachers are teaching their students in school must always hold as valid, according to the plain meanings being taught. Thus, legislating from the bench any new intent or purpose that was not put into plain expression within the text of the document is a Constitutionally-illegitimate pursuit. The sole means by which any traditional meaning of the Constitution can be legitimately altered is by means of the amendment process, with the permission of the people.

The Sixth Amendment

"That in the general distribution of powers in our system of jurisprudence, the cognizance of law belongs to the court, of fact to the jury; that as often as they are not blended, the power of the court is absolute and exclusive. That in civil cases it is always so, and may rightfully be so exerted. That in criminal cases the law and fact being always blended, the jury, for reasons of a political and peculiar nature, for the security of life and liberty, is intrusted with the power of deciding both law and fact." —Alexander Hamilton

<u>The People's Check on the Government's Power to Imprison</u>
Amendment VI to the Constitution provides the following rights to American citizens: 1) the right to a speedy and public trial; 2) an impartial jury of people from the area where the crime was committed; 3) the right of the accused to confront witnesses against him; 4) the right to force witnesses helpful to the defense to testify; and 5) the right to legal counsel.

Although the entire process outlined by the Sixth Amendment helps to protect personal property rights, within the context of accusations of criminal wrongdoing and possible incarceration, perhaps the key component of the amendment is its guarantee of a trial by jury. In many countries, the guilt or innocence of the accused is determined solely by a magistrate who works for the government. This puts the state in charge of deciding guilt or innocence, incentivizing corruption and allowing for the easy incarceration of people in disfavor with the government.

The jury system, on the other hand, provides a check on the power of the state, disallowing the easy incarceration of one's person or confiscation of one's personal property to support a state agenda or the enrichment of state agents, thus maintaining the freedom of the people. If a law, in its application, shows itself to be corrupt or unfair in the judgment of the people, a jury can always issue a finding of "not guilty" based upon the right of the jury to nullify the law. This happened with regularity, prior to the Civil War, when many juries found the helpers of escaped slaves "not guilty" in spite of laws requiring the incarceration of those individuals helping slaves to freedom. This republican right of jury nullification empowers the people to veto bad laws, on a case-by-case basis, until such time as the law might be changed. Therefore, even government-supported crimes against property can be systematically thwarted by those who choose to live in accord with republican ideals.

<u>A Short History of Jury Nullification</u>
Jury nullification—or making a finding of "not guilty" because the law used at trial is, in the eyes of the jury, unjust—has a long history in America. It began in 1670, when Quakers were tried for breaking a law permitting religious assemblies only by the authority of the Anglican Church; a jury of peers saw the injustice and acquitted them. In 1735, a jury acquitted a journalist named Zenger* who was arrested for criticizing public officials. Before the Civil War, many free-state juries refused to convict abolitionists for disobeying the Fugitive Slave Act. Nullification has also been credited with helping to end alcohol prohibition and laws prescribing harsh penalties for marijuana use. On January 1, 2013, a New Hampshire law went into effect

articulating the right of the defense to inform a jury of its right to judge not only the facts of the case in question but the application of the law. Thus, if the jury finds a law—or the method of its application—to be bad, the jury may find the defendant "not guilty as charged." (Prior to the passing of this important statute, some judges had the reputation of gagging defense lawyers with respect to jury nullification, telling them that they were not allowed to instruct juries about their right to nullify the law.)

____

*See the section of this book on the First Amendment, for more specific information on Zenger.

The Seventh Amendment

"The civil jury is a valuable safeguard to liberty." —Alexander Hamilton

Citizens' Rights in Federal Court
Amendment VII extends the right of trial by jury to federal civil cases that have at issue an amount worth more than twenty dollars, such as disputes between private parties in noncriminal matters regarding personal injuries or legal contracts. In civil cases, the person suing (the plaintiff) seeks a monetary award or a court order preventing the person sued (the defendant) from engaging in certain behavior. To win, the plaintiff must prove by a "preponderance of the evidence" the case that is before the court, which means that more than half the evidence offered must indicate wrongdoing. Since the risk of subjecting one's most valuable possession—one's body—to incarceration or execution is not present in civil cases, it is reasonable that the burden of proving the case "beyond a reasonable doubt" be lessened. This amendment also states that no factual decisions made by a jury are eligible to be overturned upon the whim of a judge, since this would basically render the power of the jury meaningless. State courts may use different rules than those prescribed in the Seventh Amendment for state civil cases that do not involve any federal rules.

President Clinton Supports the Power of the Jury
President Bill Clinton once vetoed a bill that would place caps on lawsuit damages. The reasoning was predicated on court rulings stating that caps on lawsuit damages went against the Seventh Amendment's guarantee that the jury gets to decide the facts of the case and that no statute may do so. If a jury were to find an award of a particular amount justified, then a federal statute limiting the amount to less money would be out of line with the findings of the jury and, therefore, un-Constitutional.

In a famous case, Lisa Gourley noticed one of her twins was kicking less, but her doctor said all was well. The kicking continued to lessen, so Lisa went to another doctor who rushed her to surgery for a cesarean delivery. One twin suffered extensive brain damage. An award cap in Nebraska limited Lisa's award to an amount too small to care for the affected twin for more than a few years. If a federal ground could be found for appeal, the cap would not apply in federal court.

The Amendments Continue in Their Progression From Most Personal to Most Public
So, continuing the progression from the most personal to the most public in scope, the amendments continue outward along the path from the Fifth Amendment's protection of rights in the semipublic realm (bridging the gateway from privacy rights to protections against unfair incarceration of one's person or confiscation of one's real property), moving to the protections in the Sixth Amendment for maintaining one's right to a fair public hearing by jury trial, and finally making the transition to the federal circle of influence in the Seventh Amendment. Next up: the Eighth Amendment's protection of individual rights in the least private of all situations, imprisonment by the state.

The Eighth Amendment

"Capital Punishment, a penalty regarding the justice and expediency of which many worthy persons—including all the assassins—entertain grave misgivings." —Ambrose Bierce

<u>Limits on the Government Powers to Detain & Punish</u>
Amendment VIII bars the government from charging excessive bail or imposing excessive fines. Any punishment must fit the crime. Cruel and unusual punishment is forbidden. This particular amendment carries the protection of individual rights from what is protected in the private realm all the way into the arena of what rights individuals still may maintain given a setting that is wholly divorced from the private sphere altogether. Whether the incarceration be a temporary one or one that is more permanent in nature, the individual still possesses certain unalienable rights that the government is restrained from encroaching upon.

Bail is paid to the court as an incentive for the accused to return for trial and becomes forfeit upon failure to appear. This represents, in essence, an exchange of property (in the form of money) for property (in the form of one's person). Bail promotes the concept that one is innocent until proven guilty and must be offered in an amount possible for the accused to pay. Excessive bail or fines may not be imposed, according to this amendment.

<u>Cruel & Unusual Punishment</u>
The ban on cruel and unusual punishment outlaws such things as crucifixion, drawing and quartering, and other evil acts—all crimes against one's person, the results of which may never be undone. The ban has broadened, over time, to prevent insufficient medical care of prisoners and the failure of prison officials to protect inmates from one another. There is, however, no prohibition of the death penalty, although the government has been prevented from carrying it out against juveniles or the intellectually disabled. The state cannot assign the death penalty, if such punishment does not fit the crime, nor may the state utilize a cruel or unusual method of implementing the death penalty. In a sense, this prohibition prevents unfair trades from occurring, ensuring that punishment of one's person, for a criminal act, is a *quid pro quo* exchange of value for value, penalty for misdeed.

To the Founders, the word "unusual" meant "not customary" or "contrary to long usage." Strict Constitutionalists disapprove of redefining the original meaning of the Constitution, according to an "evolving standards of decency" test, without first asking for the people's input and for their consent to any change in how the law is to be understood and applied. The Constitution is based on principles, and any specific applications are left to the people's representatives, not unelected judges. This is why, if there is no Congressional law specifically forbidding a particular practice—such as waterboarding, for instance—a president, duly elected as the representative of the whole people, may have jurisdiction in deciding whether such a practice actually constitutes a punishment which is cruel or unusual.

The Ninth Amendment

"It has been objected also against a bill of rights, that, by enumerating particular exceptions to the grant of power, it would disparage those rights which were not placed in that enumeration; and it might follow by implication, that those rights which were not singled out, were intended to be assigned into the hands of the General Government, and were consequently insecure. This is one of the most plausible arguments I have ever heard against the admission of a bill of rights into this system; but, I conceive, that it may be guarded against." —*James Madison*

<u>Rights Not Written in the Constitution Are Also Protected</u>
Amendment IX states that just because certain rights are listed in the Constitution as belonging to the people, this is not to imply that those rights are the only rights they have. There do exist Natural Rights that the people possess which, although they are not explicitly written into the Constitution, the government must respect nonetheless. These rights are referred to as "unenumerated rights."

The truth is that there are many rights the Founders did not feel the need to list, because these rights were considered to be so basic as not to be worth mentioning, such as the "right to privacy," which, although implied by the Fourth Amendment, is not explicitly mentioned. What all of this means is that the people have wide latitude in how they may behave, so long as they do not violate the property rights of others. The Ninth Amendment, according to the Constitutional principle of protecting individual rights, requires American courts to operate based upon a presumption of liberty, so that the rest of the Bill of Rights may not be used as a basis to rule out the existence of other Natural Rights belonging to the people, merely because they have not been enshrined verbally within the text of the Constitution. Thus, people are free to act, rather than being compelled to self-censor or limit their actions, so long as there be no specific mention, anywhere within the letter of the law, of any illegality posed by the action contemplated.

The Founding Fathers did not believe they were creating any new rights when they wrote the Bill of Rights. They were merely writing into law the people's most important and necessary God-given rights—or Natural Rights—as a safeguard against corruption, so that these could not so easily be infringed or voided by a future tyrannical government.

The Tenth Amendment

"Interference with the power of the States was no constitutional criterion of the power of Congress. If the power was not given, Congress could not exercise it; if given, they might exercise it, although it should interfere with the laws, or even the Constitutions, of the States."
—James Madison

The Sovereign States Hold Most Governmental Power

Amendment X holds that any government power that is not specified as being a power of the federal government rightly belongs to the states or to the people to exercise. For example, the Constitution says nothing at all about education. This means that education is an issue for the states and for the people to deal with, not the federal government. This is why there are many who believe that the very existence of the Department of Education in Washington, DC, is grossly un-Constitutional. The same goes for medical care, environmental protection, and a host of other issues not enumerated as federal responsibilities. Enforcing the Tenth Amendment would help to ensure that the people remain united on matters of national importance, since all else would be handled at the state and local levels.

The Tenth Amendment, if it were fully honored, would not mean there would be no laws made affecting healthcare, the environment, or any number of other issues of concern to voters. It means that the politics of these matters would be left to the sovereign states to settle, a reality that—if it were to exist, purely according to Constitutional guidelines—would bring much more harmony and unity to the national political scene. This would allow up to fifty different solutions to almost any given problem to be enacted in fifty different "laboratories of problem-solving." The best solutions would happily see widespread adoption, as states learned from one another. This is a much better scenario than having all the states tied to the one-size-fits-all solutions prescribed by a far-away and out-of-touch federal government. Honoring the Tenth Amendment would also mean that a large portion of the Washington bureaucracy would disappear—no more departments of Energy, Education, or Health. States would take on these issues at the less expensive and more accountable local levels. It would also shift most of the tax collections from the national to the state taxing authorities. This would make corruption harder to hide and easier to discover.

The Erosion of States' Rights

In *McCulloch v. Maryland*, Chief Justice John Marshall rejected a Tenth Amendment argument, instead choosing to enlarge the traditional interpretation of the Necessary and Proper Clause. The state counsel for Maryland voiced fears about the eventual loss of states' rights, and tried to use the Tenth Amendment to argue against this, in order to support his claim that the power to create corporations was reserved, by the Tenth Amendment, to the sovereign states. Marshall, however, declared that, since the amendment—unlike the similarly worded Articles of Confederation on this issue—omitted the word "expressly" as a qualifier, the entire question was left open as to "whether the particular power which may become the subject of contest has been delegated to the one government, or prohibited to the other. . . ." (The Tenth Amendment, in its entirety, reads like this: "The powers not delegated to the United States by the Constitution, nor prohibited by it to the states, are reserved to the states respectively, or to the people.")

Many have, to be sure, lamented over Marshall's invention of an absent word*, the leaving out of which might constitute grounds for a reinterpretation of the amendment as the Founders obviously chose to write it; for this has left open to the federal government more room for mischief in how the federal government might choose to justify the usurpation of state authority. Although Marshall had a brilliant mind, perhaps he used it too much in favor of enabling government encroachment, rather than defending the people's rights against infringement.

____

*Read more about the juridical mischief-making of John Marshall in Appendix C.

Appendix A: The Battle of Athens: Armed Citizenry as a Necessary Check Against Tyranny

"It is the responsibility of the patriot to protect his country from its government."
—Thomas Paine

<u>Corruption in McMinn County</u>
On August 1st and 2nd of 1946, patriotic Americans used armed force to ensure a fair outcome in local elections. Voter fraud was running rampant, with forged ballots and secret vote counts commonplace. Federal authorities were asked to intervene, but the calls for oversight fell on deaf ears.

<u>Fighting Tyranny Abroad & at Home</u>
Many calling for the abolition of corruption, and the tyranny it was breeding, were World War Two veterans whose wartime experiences made them determined not to have fought against tyranny abroad, only to find it lurking in their communities of Athens and Etowah, Tennessee.

<u>Unwelcome Competition</u>
Paul Cantrell was elected sheriff three times back-to-back, in '36, '38, and '40, and elected state senator in '42 and '44. Cantrell's associate, Pat Mansfield, was elected sheriff in his stead during Cantrell's senate years. And, in 1946, Cantrell decided that he wanted to be elected sheriff once again.

But, at the end of 1945, some 3,000 veterans, seasoned by hard fighting in the European and Pacific theaters of war, returned home to McMinn County. These veterans decided to put up one of their own to run as a candidate for sheriff in the primary election against Cantrell. These ex-GIs promised honest elections to the voters as a part of their reform plan for the county government, in which the sheriff played a key role. Other GIs stood for election as well.

<u>Bullets to Guarantee Ballots</u>
During the August 1st primary election, 200 armed men were brought in by political leaders to act as "deputies" at the polls. GI poll-watchers were beaten by these men. At 3:00 PM, Tom Gillespie, a black man, was told by a deputy not to vote. When Gillespie persisted, he was shot, and a crowd gathered. The rumor that ran through the town was that Gillespie had been shot in the back! (Gillespie eventually recovered.)

Poll-watchers were not allowed into the area where ballots were to be counted, and Sheriff Mansfield ordered his "deputies" to disperse the public. One of the deputies raised his gun and called out, "If you sons of bitches cross this street I'll kill you!"

The GIs decided to find themselves some appropriate weaponry for the situation and thereby take matters into their own hands. The National Guard and State Guard armories had American M-1 rifles, British Enfield rifles, and some .45 caliber pistols.

The Battle of Athens
GIs were fired upon from the jail, as they warned people to get away for their own safety. Two GIs were hit. Without proper communications, the GIs found it difficult to coordinate their attack on the jail, in the gun battle that ensued. Some citizens were wounded on the street, and one of Mansfield's men inside the jail was shot as well.

By 2:00 AM, on August 2nd, the GIs had decided to throw some dynamite, damaging the jail's porch, and the deputies surrendered. The GIs took control of the jail and held the deputies there overnight, until calm was restored to the town. The GIs cleaned and returned the guns they had borrowed to the armories. With the ballots counted transparently in full view of the public, the GI candidate for sheriff, Knox Henry, won his election—and other GI candidates won as well— by a 3-to-2 margin.

After the Test Comes the Lesson
The Battle of Athens demonstrates how American patriots can restore the rule of law, by legitimately ousting corrupt, scofflaw politicians by force of arms. America's Founders saw the entire American people as being a standing militia, ready to defend their freedom from invasion or against tyranny. Indeed, the Second Amendment to the US Constitution reads thus: "A well regulated Militia being necessary to the security of a free State, the right of the people to keep and bear Arms shall not be infringed."

Thomas Jefferson, upon expressing the American philosophy of governance in the words of the Declaration of Independence, wrote the following: "We hold these truths to be self-evident, that all men are created equal, that they are endowed by their Creator with certain unalienable Rights, that among these are Life, Liberty and the pursuit of Happiness. —That to secure these rights, Governments are instituted among Men, deriving their just powers from the consent of the governed, —That *whenever any Form of Government becomes destructive of these ends, it is the Right of the People to alter or to abolish it, and to institute new Government*, laying its foundation on such principles and organizing its powers in such form, as to them shall seem most likely to effect their Safety and Happiness." It was this principle in action that the World War Two veterans of Athens, Tennessee, were executing.

In America's Declaration of Independence, 27 complaints against the British Crown are outlined, framed in terms of an American philosophy of Natural Rights. But the Golden-Rule-based solutions to righting the wrongs complained about do not find proper expression until the framing of the Constitution, which stands as a blueprint for freedom across time and space.

The Battle of Athens remains a spirited example of what good, patriotic Americans can do to protect their fellows from government tyranny. It is a lesson Americans should never forget.

———

At the time of this book's publication, a dramatization of the Battle of Athens was available at YouTube.com, in a short enactment entitled "The Battle of Athens: Restoring the Rule of Law" (https://www.youtube.com/watch?time_continue=23&v=U5ut6yPrObw).

Appendix B: How the Electoral College Places Freedom Above Majority Rule

"Direct election would break down the federal system under which states entered the union, which provides a system of checks and balances to ensure that no area or group shall obtain too much power." —John F. Kennedy

The Distributive Wisdom of the Electoral College
The Electoral College was wisely created by the Framers of the Constitution, in order to privilege the votes of the state elections in importance, over and above the nationwide popular vote. It must be remembered that the states created the federal government, and not the other way around, so the statewide elections take precedence in an election where the states get to choose the president, not the people directly. To protect small states from being always ruled by the interests of large states, the Electoral College incorporated protection of the minority into the election of the president by adding the number of representatives and senators together to determine the number of Electors for each state. Thus, Rhode Island receives three electoral votes, rather than one; this means the state's balance of power becomes 3/535, rather than the 1/435 ratio of a direct-proportion-of-the-population model. It is plain to see how small states can elect their presidential choice, in spite of a national popular vote count favoring the big states' preferred candidate. The impact of this reality on the larger states is that it limits their capacity to exercise an unreasonable degree of power over the smaller states.

Because the states choose the president by their electoral votes—rather than the people electing the president directly—the president is not called President of the American People, but is referred to, instead, as President of the United States. So, here is how the Electoral College worked to protect the minority in the presidential election of 2016:

Donald Trump received the majority of votes in 2,623 counties. Hillary Clinton won in only 489. Trump also won in 30 states and in one of Maine's Congressional districts. (Maine awards its electors differently, one for each Congressional district independently, and two for the winner of the statewide election.) This made Trump, by far, the preferred choice of most countywide and statewide jurisdictions within the United States.

After the votes were all totaled, however, it became apparent that Clinton had won the national popular vote by close to 2.9 million votes. However, the state of California preferred Clinton by a margin of 2 to 1 over Trump (61.5% to 31.5%), with Clinton winning by a margin of 4 million votes in California, a margin exceeding, by more than a million votes, the national margin by which she won the national popular vote.

This means that *one state's* popular votes were able to swing the national popular vote quite dramatically. But should the interests and concerns of one area of the country, as idiosyncratic as California, choose the president by its popular vote margin alone? This demonstrates how important the Electoral College is in protecting the rights of the minority by distributing the power to elect the president in a way that helps protect the interests of the smaller states. Under the American system, the less populous states can succeed in electing their preference for president, regardless of his lack of popularity in a huge population center like California.

The Founders' model for nationwide presidential elections forces distribution of the power to elect a chief executive for the entire country to a variety of places far and wide. The Electoral College ensures that diverse regional points of view come into play in electing the president, rather than allowing one homogenous population center alone to make such an important choice. When it comes to the Electoral College, diversity is guaranteed, and the rights of the minority are protected.

A Protection Against Corruption

Also, the Electoral College's safeguard against one corrupt state's ability to tip the national popular vote—rather than just the vote within the confines of its own borders—is just as valuable today as ever. Without the Electoral College, if one state runs up the national vote total for a particular candidate, by means of allowing corruption at the polling places, the entire country could be forced to live with a candidate who was in no way the legitimate choice of the American people.

A Warning From Malcolm X

Malcolm X once said the following about the Chicago political machine: "In Chicago, the Precinct Captains watch to see who votes and who doesn't. Then, at the end of the day, others will cast votes for those who haven't shown up to vote, all under the direction of the Precinct Captain. If the actual voter shows up later, they're given someone else's card." Malcolm X is also known to have said, "In Chicago, the Precinct Captain sometimes goes into the polling booth to make sure the ghost voter votes correctly, making sure they pull the right lever, if they aren't that bright. Even pulling it for them." And, with regard to absentee ballots, he made this statement: "In Chicago, in every election, there are many absentee ballots, and a lot of them are sent in by Precinct Captains, or by someone associated with the campaign."

The National Popular Vote Plan: How It Might Sponsor Corruption at the Polling Place

Chief executives of twelve states (DC is included in the count, although it is not a state) have signed the National Popular Vote Plan (NPVP) into law. According to the plan, these jurisdictions all agree to award their presidential electoral votes to the candidate who wins the national popular vote, rather than the popular votes of their own states. The NPVP has been passed into law by twelve states, possessing 172 electoral votes, at the time of this writing (CA, CT, DC, HI, IL, MA, MD, NJ, NY, RI, VT, & WA). It takes effect once states possessing 270 electoral votes pass the statute.

However, any given state's lack of a voter-ID law—which encourages illegal voting—would mean that the state's illegal votes would have the potential to tip the national popular vote in favor of the rightful loser. This could compel the NPVP states—in spite of who rightfully won the popular votes in those states—to award their electoral votes to the winner of the now-fraudulent national vote. What a miscarriage of justice such an election would be! States with voter-ID laws would be fighting voter fraud in vain, while many other states, potentially, would be running up the vote totals illegally (Chicago-style), in order to rig the election.

Dishonesty Wins!
The more corrupt a state is with regard to abetting illegal voters, the more the cheating would help the party favored by the majority of fraudulent voters. Dishonesty would tend to win out over honesty almost every time, in such an environment. Thus, one unsavory result of the NPVP could be that the very incentive for preserving integrity could disappear, as honest states determine it to be in their best electoral interests to behave the same way that dishonest states behave—which might easily lead to corruption beyond the ability of the public to repair!

California Corruption
California claims that 78% of its eligible voters are actually registered to vote, but polling watchdog Linda Paine, of the Election Integrity Project of California, says the figure is actually much higher, once the inactive voters are factored in, bringing that percentage to 98%! (Eight of California's 58 counties actually have more than 100% voter-registration rates, based on figures from February 10, 2017, on Secretary of State Alex Padilla's official website). And when 5 million inactive voters, who have died or moved to another state, are brought into the mix, in light of California's lack of a voter-ID requirement, the risk of voter fraud abounds, especially since many California counties combine the lists of active and inactive voters together for the polling places on election day. It is also true, according to Linda Paine, that people who report the passing away of their loved ones to have them removed from California's voter rolls are typically met with non-action, their loved ones remaining on the rolls for many years to come.

The Election Integrity Project of Judicial Watch has also said, concurrently with Linda Paine in 2017, that the US has 3.5 million more voters on the election rolls than are alive in the adult population, according to data from the US Census Bureau's 2011–2015 American Community Survey and the Election Assistance Commission. This is largely due to maintenance of inactive voter rolls across the country, which means that many citizens might easily be double- or even triple-registered, depending on their mobility and how many times they may have moved over the last two presidential election cycles. This indicates a problem with a great potential for electoral abuse.

Chicago-Style Machines
Before the NPVP was formulated, the capacity of the Electoral College to act as a safeguard against corruption was never in doubt. If passed by enough states, however, there would exist significant incentives to stuff ballot boxes and allow illegal voting that, before the plan took effect, would not have been worth the risks. The value of the Electoral College as a stop against corruption would become non-existent.

All the potential dishonesty that could be unleashed would mean that, regardless of how well a candidate campaigned, the hard work would not matter on Election Day. The only thing that would matter, in the end, would be how well the political machines of each state operated to skew the vote counts in favor of illegally pre-chosen candidates. If the candidates knew that the people would not have the power to choose the winner, they would become more preoccupied with Chicago-style behind-the-scenes machinations than with making open promises to the people. This would pose serious problems for the survival of the United States as a free republic.

<u>The Loss of Representative Government</u>
The NPVP could spell the end of integrity in the American electoral system. Only the cheaters would prevail. The valid choice elected by the sovereign states might never be known for sure, ever again. The people would not get the president they deserve, with protections for the minority to limit the power of the majority, as envisioned by America's Founders. The loss of America's free republic would be a *fait accompli*.

Appendix C: Constitutional Supremacy Versus Judicial Supremacy

"You seem . . . to consider the judges as the ultimate arbiters of all constitutional questions; a very dangerous doctrine indeed, and one which would place us under the despotism of an oligarchy. Our judges are as honest as other men, and not more so. They have, with others, the same passions for party, for power, and the privilege of their corps. . . . [T]heir power [is] the more dangerous as they are in office for life, and not responsible, as the other functionaries are, to the elective control. The Constitution has erected no such single tribunal, knowing that to whatever hands confided, with the corruptions of time and party, its members would become despots. It has more wisely made all the departments co-equal and co-sovereign within themselves. If the legislature fails to pass laws . . . as prescribed by the constitution, or if they fail to meet in congress, the judges cannot issue their mandamus* *to them; if the President fails to provide the place of a judge, . . . the judges cannot force him. They can issue their* mandamus *or* distringas** *to no executive or legislative officer to enforce the fulfilment of their official duties, any more than the president or legislature may issue orders to judges or their officers."*
—Thomas Jefferson's Letter to Mr. Jarvis, dated September 28, 1820, at Monticello, wherein he affirms the co-equal powers of the branches of government

Marbury v. Madison: Background

Just before the end of President John Adams' term as president, Adams appointed 16 Federalist judges to the federal circuit courts and another 42 jurists to lesser courts. This action was allowed, due to late passage of a statute called the Judiciary Act of 1801, which doubled the number of court circuits from three to six and loaded them with Federalists, in an attempt to thwart the incoming Democratic Republicans. These judicial appointments became known as the "Midnight Judges." Although the new judgeships were hastily approved, and the nominees to the posts were expeditiously ratified by the lame-duck Senate, the commissions to these posts had to be delivered to the individual appointees to become official. The job of carrying out the delivery of these commissions fell to John Marshall, who, although he had recently been appointed Chief Justice of the Supreme Court, was still busy fulfilling his duties as the acting Secretary of State for President Adams. Although Marshall succeeded in delivering a majority of the commissions to the intended recipients, the clock ran out when Thomas Jefferson was sworn in as the new president.

One of the first acts by Jefferson as chief executive was to cancel delivery of the remaining commissions, which would include canceling the delivery of a commission to one William Marbury. According to Jefferson's point of view, the commissions, having not been delivered on time, were null and void. And Jefferson's new government, dominated by his own party, would eventually proceed with repealing the Judiciary Act of 1801, thereby ridding the federal judiciary of a host of Federalist judges. As remedy, Marbury took his case to the Supreme Court, to force the Jefferson Administration to deliver him his commission.

<u>*Marbury v. Madison*: the Case</u>
On February 24, 1803, the Supreme Court ruled unanimously that Marbury had the right to his commission but that the Court had no power to force the delivery of it. So, in short, John Marshall, now the sitting Chief Justice, wrote, in his legal opinion, that the non-delivery of the commission violated the law; also, the laws of the United States did offer Marbury a legal remedy in his dispute; but the Court did not have the legal jurisdiction to issue a *Writ of Mandamus* to force the executive branch to comply with the law. In other words, there was a legal remedy already available that did not require an intervention by the Supreme Court. This being the end of the matter, nothing more was legally required to be said.

<u>*Obiter Dictum* or Enduring Principle?</u>
However, Marshall refused to bring the matter to an end, going on to explain that, in his view, the Judiciary Act of 1789's assigning of jurisdiction to the Supreme Court, for the issuing of a legal remedy like the one being requested by Marbury, was in conflict with Article III of the Constitution, which clearly defined the Supreme Court's original and appellate jurisdictions, and which did not include this extra one assigned by Congress. Marshall was saying that Congress had no authority to modify the Supreme Court's original jurisdiction. So, since the Court had before it a conflict between a federal law and the Constitution, Marshall had decided that, in such an instance, the Court must side with the Constitution, finding any act of Congress that came into conflict with the Constitution to be un-Constitutional and, therefore, not law. In other words, Marshall had just declared, definitively, and in writing, that the Supreme Court was the proper authority in deciding all questions of Constitutionality, among the three branches of government.

Marshall opined, in writing, the following *obiter dictum****: "[I]f both the law and the Constitution apply to a particular case, so that the Court must either decide that case conformably to the law, disregarding the Constitution, or conformably to the Constitution, disregarding the law, the Court must determine which of these conflicting rules governs the case. This is of the very essence of judicial duty. If, then, the Courts are to regard the Constitution, and the Constitution is superior to any ordinary act of the Legislature, the Constitution, and not such ordinary act, must govern the case to which they both apply." So, by ruling that it had no jurisdiction to hear this case assigned to it by an act of Congress, due to a conflict between that act and the Constitution, the Supreme Court had now established itself to be the final word on the meaning of the Constitution, in the eyes of many. However, there was no universal agreement in this regard. There were, in fact, many who refused to agree on this point.

<u>Jefferson's Viewpoint</u>
Indeed, Thomas Jefferson wrote in his Letter to Judge Johnson, dated June 12, 1823, at Monticello (per *Memoir, Correspondence, and Miscellanies, from the Papers of Thomas Jefferson*, edited by Thomas Jefferson Randolph), that "[t]his practice of Judge Marshall, of travelling out of his case to prescribe what the law would be in a moot case not before the court, is very irregular and very censurable . . . [since] the Chief Justice went on to lay down what the law would be, had they jurisdiction of the case; to wit, that they should command this delivery. The object was clearly to instruct any other court having the jurisdiction, what they should do, if

Marbury should apply to them. Besides the impropriety of this gratuitous interference, could any thing exceed the perversion of law?" Jefferson sees Marshall as having clearly gone beyond the scope of his role as Chief Justice.

Moreover, Jefferson writes, "[W]hatever is in the executive offices is certainly deemed to be in the hands of the President; and, in this case, was actually in my hands, because, when I countermanded them, there was as yet no Secretary of State. Yet this case of Marbury and Madison is continually cited by bench and bar, as if it were settled law, without any animadversion [censorious comment] on its being merely an *obiter* [incidental] dissertation of the Chief Justice." It is clear that Jefferson believes that, since the Court lacked jurisdiction and admitted as much, any other commentary upon this matter should be of no legal consequence. Once the Supreme Court quit the case, it did not have authority to go on. The case was closed at the moment the Court found there was no jurisdiction. Any further commentary was merely extra-legal and incidental, without applicable legal value. Further, Jefferson seems to propose that the executive has just as much right to interpret the Constitution as the judicial branch does. This would also suggest that the same is true of the legislative branch. According to Jefferson's notion expressed here, each of the three branches has a say in how the Constitution is to be interpreted. And the Supreme Court is not the ultimate arbiter of Constitutional interpretation; indeed, it is the American people who must have the final word.

Jefferson continues: "But the Chief Justice says, 'there must be an ultimate arbiter somewhere.' True, there must; but does that prove it is either party? The ultimate arbiter is the people of the Union, assembled by their deputies in convention, at the call of Congress, or of two thirds of the States [per Article V of the Constitution]. Let them decide to which they mean to give an authority claimed by two of their organs. And it has been the peculiar wisdom and felicity of our constitution, to have provided this peaceable appeal, where that of other nations is at once to force." It is obvious that the Jeffersonian ideal is one where the people decide the issue, per the amendment process laid out in Article V of the Constitution.

<u>Abe Lincoln Asserts Constitutional Supremacy over Judicial Supremacy</u>
In a book review of *The Constitution: An Introduction*, appearing in the *Washington Post* on May 20, 2015, Michael S. Paulsen discusses the tension between "Constitutional supremacy" and "judicial supremacy." Republican candidate Abraham Lincoln stood for the former notion, while Stephen Douglas—his Democrat opponent in a series of seven debates, during their now-famous 1858 contest for the Senate—stood for the latter. According to Paulsen, "Lincoln stood for constitutional supremacy, and against the prospective binding authority of the Supreme Court's betrayal of the Constitution in *Dred Scott v. Sandford.* . . . [I]t seems fair to say that one cannot embrace the modern view of reflexive judicial supremacy without simultaneously opposing nearly everything Lincoln said and did as President. Indeed, on a thoroughgoing judicial supremacist view, it could fairly be argued that the South was justified in seceding—in reaction to the election of a president committed to a lawless course of action. . . . Lincoln's position on slavery in the territories and the Supreme Court's decision in *Dred Scott* were in direct contradiction. Today it seems clear that Lincoln's interpretation of the Constitution was

right and the Supreme Court's interpretation was wrong—horribly, willfully wrong. Yet, was Lincoln not bound to regard the Supreme Court's decision against his position as deciding the matter? Indeed, are not all public officials, and all citizens, obliged to treat the Court's decisions as settling constitutional questions, whether they agree with those decisions or not?" Lincoln's argument was that the Supreme Court's opinions are only binding upon the outcome of each case set before it; they were non-binding on the President of the United States and on the Congress. Thus, unlawful rulings by the Court may be legally ignored by the executive and legislative branches until such time as those harmful decisions are finally reversed or overturned in favor of Constitutional ones. Lincoln insisted that this was part of the Constitution's system of checks and balances. "The alternative, in Lincoln's mind, was resignation of free, popular government under the Constitution into the hands of the Court, no matter how wrongheaded its decisions." And popular sovereignty, according to the letter and the spirit of the Constitution, was never intended to yield to a judicial-based system of elitist oligarchy, wherein a relative few elites in black robes dictate law by legislating from the bench.

Other Cases Where the Supreme Court Got It Wrong
Two other cases, besides *Dred Scott*, where the Supreme Court went totally off the rails, by ruling into law Constitutional rights without any basis at all in the Constitution itself, are *Roe v. Wade* and *Obergefell v. Hodges*. Both rulings were out of line with Constitutional principles.

The Court ruled on *Roe*, in 1973, finding that a woman had a Constitutional right to an abortion. Since the Constitution does not address anything close to reproductive rights anywhere in its text—which is a no-brainer to anyone who cares to read its 4,440 plain words—abortion becomes a Tenth Amendment issue, left for the states to decide, not the federal judiciary. The correct ruling would have been for the Court to have ruled that there was no federal jurisdiction in the matter. In the case of *Obergefell*, over four decades later, the Court ruled that gay marriage was a Constitutional right. The problem is that, once again, this issue is properly left to the states to decide; the Constitution is mum with regard to the institution of marriage.

Why Constitutional Supremacy Needs to Be Affirmed
While many people were cheering for the outcomes which came about, even those people are hurt by these bad Supreme Court rulings in the long run, for the setting of any precedent that the Supreme Court has the right to make new laws for the people, outside of the regular legislative process, robs the people—all of the people—of their right to decide what laws they want for themselves, through their elected representatives. All that is needed for the federal court system to evolve into an unelected oligarchy—a set of likeminded rulers, 90% of whom have graduated from the same small coterie of law schools—is for the people to accept, time and again, this brand of judicial overreach. It is nothing new. And it has been vigorously opposed by Thomas Jefferson, Abraham Lincoln, and many others. If the American people do not rise in opposition to judicial supremacy whenever it occurs—but instead choose to habituate themselves to the practice—they ultimately risk losing their freedom, as the legislative choices they make to govern their lives, through their chosen representatives, will be nullified time and again by

unelected elites in black robes. In the end, Constitutional supremacy must be affirmed, lest the American people risk losing their free republic.

------

*_Mandamus_ = A _Writ of Mandamus_ is judicial order from a superior court to any lower court, public official, or public authority to do—or cease from doing—some specific act which is a public duty, and, in certain instances, one of a statutory duty.
**_Distringas_ = A _Writ of Distringas_ is a legal paper commanding the sheriff of the county in which a defendant resides, or owns any goods, to seize property of the defendant to compel the defendant's appearance, especially in cases wherein it is impracticable to get the defendant personally in order to serve a summons upon him.
***_Obiter dictum_ = An _obiter dictum_ is an incidental opinion that bears only passing relevance to the matter at hand.

Appendix D: Why Free Speech Is So Vital in a Free Republic

"To suppress free speech is a double wrong. It violates the rights of the hearer as well as those of the speaker." —Frederick Douglass

<u>The Responsible Exercise of Freedom: The Big Lie about "Safe Spaces"</u>
The big lie that "safe spaces" exist that will guarantee emotional security must be vigorously debunked in a free republic. It is important to disabuse the foes of free speech of the naïve notion that banning free speech somehow makes people safe. Indeed, the opposite is true. Totalitarian socialist regimes have ofttimes criminalized speech, but, rather than just stopping all of the outlawed speech, what they have most dramatically accomplished is the incarceration—as well as the execution—of dissenters. Even many who were on the side of the State, to begin with, may at times run afoul of the very speech codes that they once supported.

<u>"No One Left to Speak Out"</u>
The most famous illustration of the fallacy of supporting—either actively or by passive acceptance—the policies of a freedom-killing State is perhaps the one espoused by Martin Niemöller with regard to Hitler's National Socialist German Workers Party: "First they came for the Communists, and I did not speak out—because I was not a Communist. Next they came for the Social Democrats, and I did not speak out—because I was not a Social Democrat. Then they came for the Trade Unionists, and I did not speak out—because I was not a Trade Unionist. Then they came for the Jews, and I did not speak out—because I was not a Jew. Then they came for me—and there was no one left to speak out."*

<u>The Intolerance of the Deadly Isms Begins on Campus & Enters the Culture</u>
Martin Niemöller, a pastor who spoke out against Hitler, spent seven years in concentration camps. And let there be no doubt, incarceration is what many socialists would love to inflict on the supporters of full-throated free speech, because socialism only works by means of government force, and socialists are never tolerant of their critics, eventually forcing their compliance at the point of a gun. Back in the 1960s, in the name of diversity, colleges and universities began hiring Marxist faculty members. It is, however, pure folly for any university to zealously promote the deadly ideology of Marxism, which has, in its various forms (socialism, communism, fascism, et al.), claimed a total of more than 100 million lives in less than 100 years. It is ironic that academic communities in support of these deadly isms have now grown to the exclusion of almost all other voices on a majority of college and university faculties; their teachings of intolerance for any speech other than politically-correct expressions of "social justice" (a modern socialist dogma) has produced many weak-minded graduates who seem incapable of independent thought or the ability to argue and debate rationally and with civility. And these intolerant "social justice warriors" are graduating from many of the institutions that have historically been counted among America's finest colleges and universities.

Teaching students the truth about socialism in all its deadly forms is important; but it seems that this is something that the socialists themselves are not wont to do, preferring instead to promote the fallacy that, if only socialism were done the proper way, it would be a boon and a blessing to everyone. But socialism has been tried again and again in different iterations, and it has never worked, because people must give up all individual rights in their submission to the collective. And once this has occurred, the majority always becomes so powerful and the minority so weak that no one is safe from the tyranny of the collective. Human nature does not change, and absolute power for any one group always leads to evil outcomes for those who are not in agreement with them.   To see real-life examples of this truth, one need go no further than a college or university campus.

<u>The Thought Police Flourish on Campus, Denying Speech Rights & Claiming Privileges</u>
It has become the job of "social justice warriors" on college campuses to act as Orwellian thought police and, as such, to vigorously enforce speech codes and shut down "micro-aggressions," even to the point of bullying and violence. Wearing a sombrero, if one is not Latino, might get one labeled racist, for example, for committing the micro-aggression of "cultural appropriation," something once regarded as an expression of acceptance or flattery of the culture being emulated. It used to be acceptable for a student to dress up as someone of a different culture for a costume party, for example, but the current ethic from the Ivy League to the University of California System disallows this, lest the costumed person be accused of the micro-aggression of racist cultural appropriation, even to the point of coming under physical attack. A fun and creative exercise in freedom of expression has thus been deemed a form of bigotry, regardless of context, according to the ideology of social justice. All of these rules are socially *prescriptive* and authoritarian, disallowing the actors involved the *descriptive* right or freedom to define themselves differently or to explain how what they meant was not racist. Social justice warriors deny the *right* of the individual to explain, claiming, instead, that only members of the social justice collective are endowed with the *privilege* of getting to define what was meant by someone else's actions, even if they have no access to the mind or imagination of the actor. This is pure prejudice, pure intolerance, pure arrogance; and it runs counter to all notions of fairness in a civil society that protects individual and minority rights.

<u>Ideology of Intolerance: It Is What Many College Professors & Media Outlets Teach Nowadays</u>
This ideology of intolerance has not confined itself solely to college campuses; it is being espoused nowadays by the propagandists working for America's national conspiracy media. Due to bullying by advocates of social justice, Scarlett Johansson announced, in the summer of 2018, that she would give up her opportunity to play the role of a transgender character in a movie entitled *Rub and Tug*, due to complaints from social justice activists. "In light of recent ethical questions raised surrounding my casting as Dante Tex Gill, I have decided to respectfully withdraw my participation in the project," Johansson announced, in an effort to transform herself from villain into hero, by claiming she has "learned a lot from the [transgender] community since making my first statement about my casting and realize it was insensitive." Johansson's crime was the serious micro-aggression, in the eyes of social justice warriors, of acting in the role of a transgender person, although only transgender actors and actresses should be allowed the

privilege to play such a part. (The identity politics of social justice dictates privileges; it does not allow freedom.)

Acting is all about pretending to be someone else, someone different from the actor, often learning something in the process, by the free expression of one's creativity. So, does Ms. Johansson's withdrawal from the role mean that transgender actors should also be banned from playing non-transgender roles? From the point of view of freedom, the answer is this: Every actor should be allowed to perform any role that the actor is capable of pulling off. (And Scarlett Johansson might actually learn something by playing the role in question that transgender people already know and do not need to learn by playing such a part.)

<u>Protecting Offensive Speech Is Valued Among the Members of Civil Society in a Free Republic</u>
In America, even if a person's speech is offensive, that speech is protected by the First Amendment! The proper remedy for offensive speech—and this cannot be overemphasized—is an abundance of inoffensive speech. Indeed, how are the fallacious ideas of others to be improved or corrected, if we do not allow them to speak at all, so that we may disabuse them of problematic or counterfactual notions? And how are we to be disabused of our own faulty ideas, if we do not let others speak up, in order to point out to us where the problems lie in our own thinking? The absence of discourse perpetuates divisiveness and the continuance of faulty or objectionable reasoning—on both sides—that could have been reframed along more tenable lines or more well-informed ways of thinking. So, free speech makes all participants in civil society much wiser, as long as they are willing to understand one another within a framework of polite listening and civil discourse. Even if two parties of incompatible mindsets can simply agree to disagree, that is a civilized outcome that promotes harmony and understanding. Respect for the other viewpoint is a cherished value that can only be learned where a civil society is present. And being able to cooperate with others, despite differences of opinion, is a hallmark of a free republic where the rights of minorities are protected and intolerance enjoys no sanction.

<u>The Notion of Offensive Speech Is Subjective</u>
The entire notion of offensive speech is subjective. What one person finds offensive another person finds harmless. The very *raison d'être* of the First Amendment is to protect offensive speech, since agreeable speech needs no protection. Statists have argued repeatedly in favor of government rules to protect Americans against "hate speech." But this begs the question: What is hate speech? Was Bill Maher's televised comment that he was a "house nigga," hate speech? What about Kathy Griffin's mock-beheading of President Donald Trump? And what about Stephen Colbert's depiction of presidential advisor Steve Miller's decapitated head on a pike? Should these people be fined or imprisoned for their "hate speech"?

<u>One Person's Joke Is Another's Insult</u>
As offensive as some instances of free expression might be, such speech is not illegal under the Constitution; and what is humorous to some (for example, to hardcore fans of Maher, Griffin, or Colbert) can be offensive to others. Whether or not the expressive acts previously referenced represent "hate speech" is arguable; Maher's comments were politically motivated and not

maliciously directed against black people; Griffin's pseudo-beheading of Trump was also politically motivated; and the same goes for Colbert's simulation of Steve Miller's decapitated head on a pike. It is likely that Maher never would have made his comment outside the specific context of his show, and Griffin and Colbert probably would never have decapitated Trump and Miller, in effigy, if not for political reasons. But whatever anyone may think of such brutal shtick, imprisonment should never be an actual consequence for its performance—although social consequences may well be expected, or, in some cases, even deserved. Indeed, who would have the privilege of making the rules surrounding what constitutes "hate speech"? Since "hate speech" is typically minority speech (otherwise there would not exist the majority agreement needed to target the speech so designated), it would always require an act of majority oppression to ban such speech.

Transparency Requires Freedom of Speech
Another reason not to ban "hate speech"—other than preserving the freedom of those expressing minority views—is so Americans do not delude themselves about the existence of certain views. If racist speech is banned, Americans might easily be fooled into believing that racism no longer exists. As long as free speech exists, the airing of unexpurgated truth, warts and all, cannot be avoided. And, in a free society, if one is offended, then one is always free not to listen and free to disbelieve what one has heard.

Another case in favor of freedom of expression is to be found in Hans Christian Andersen's parable, "The Emperor's New Clothes." In the story, only the little boy who speaks freely— saying, "But he isn't wearing anything at all!"—actually reveals the truth, while all who feel constrained in their speech choose to lie out of fear. The moral to the story is this: People without freedom of expression are often required to lie to protect themselves. This leads to a culture of ignorance and deceit. It was such a culture that led to the big lies and fake news published daily in Russia's *Pravda* and *Izvestia*, during the time of the USSR (the Union of Soviet Socialist Republics). And it is the same kind of political culture that is infecting American media outlets in the late 20th and early 21st centuries—the culture of political correctness, whose adherents limit their thoughts to culturally-prescribed notions of the same anti-freedom culture that once held sway in socialist Russia.

Khrushchev's Prediction
Less than a year before Random House published Ayn Rand's *Atlas Shrugged*, Nikita Khrushchev, on November 18, 1956, famously said, "We [socialists] will take America without firing a shot. We do not have to invade the US. We will destroy you from within." Rand's perceptive reading of the anti-freedom news-media mindset, depicted in her novel, was prescient in its day, recognizing the presence of, and predicting the blossoming of, the culture of *Pravda* and *Izvestia* on American shores—a culture in which not even the American Newspaper of Record, *The New York Times*, could be trusted to practice freedom of speech in its editorial policies anymore, let alone practice true journalism, devoid of political agendas.

Free Speech: Necessary for Truth
Free speech brings out the truth, as long as that truth can get a public airing and the people remain free to see it printed or to hear it spoken. The situation in America, at the time of this book's publication, is one that is fraught with peril, from the perspective of those who love

freedom of speech, since only half a dozen media giants (CBS, Comcast, Disney, News Corp, Warner Media, and Viacom) control 90% of "news" outlets. This is very unhealthy in terms of promoting pluralism in thought. Too much information—and disinformation—is controlled by the few, the danger being the straightjacketing of thought by an overabundance of media "groupthink."

So how can one tell if a news outlet is offering fact-based reportage or fake news? Real news sites report on everything that is newsworthy without omitting critical information, such as problems that are politically-incorrect to discuss, like Europe's problems with migrant rape gangs, how East Anglia University was used as a clearing house for sharing doctored global-warming data, or how Al Gore leaves a carbon footprint way larger than most Americans (which would beg the question of whether Gore does honestly believe in global warming, if he willingly pollutes the atmosphere far more than what he would call "one's fair share"). Real news sites even report on fake news itself, backing up their information by using sourced quotes and accurately written citations, rather than anonymous sources and misleadingly edited information.

<u>New Media</u>
Opposed to the legacy media that specialize in conspiratorial reporting to promote a political agenda, the New Media have arisen to inject factual reporting and fresh perspectives into the stale narrative of elite corporatism that has so cleverly and carefully effected the hijacking of 90% or more of America's news. A partial list of a few New Media information sources might go like this: *Breitbart News, CNS News, The Gateway Pundit, The Federalist, The Daily Caller, Eagle Rising,* and *Townhall.* The common characteristic of these sources is that none of them are bound by political-correctness or loyalty to the narratives to which other media outlets so slavishly conform, and all of them have been smeared and targeted by Big Data companies attempting to censor them and limit their ability to compete. Freedom is the watchword, as opposed to self-censorship or groupthink. Diversity of thought is prized. Anyone who is in favor of closing down media outlets demonstrates an anti-freedom worldview. Beware those people who disparage diversity of thought and the discovery or enjoyment of alternative sources of information. A free republic depends on freedom and education, not censorship and indoctrination. What is taught in the pedagogy of a free republic is *how* to think and evaluate for oneself, and never *what* to think in accord with some narrative. Good ideas win out by being argued for, not by being forced on people. Do not trust one media site exclusively, but always do research when it comes to important issues. When free speech exists, the truth will out.

-----

*Als die Nazis die Kommunisten holten,
habe ich geschwiegen;
ich war ja kein Kommunist.

Als sie die Sozialdemokraten einsperrten,
habe ich geschwiegen;
ich war ja kein Sozialdemokrat.

Als sie die Gewerkschafter holten,
habe ich nicht protestiert;
ich war ja kein Gewerkschafter.

Als sie die Juden holten,
habe ich geschwiegen;
ich war ja kein Jude.

Als sie mich holten,
gab es keinen mehr,
der protestieren konnte.

Appendix E: Charlton Heston's Pro-Second-Amendment Speech at the National Press Club

"The laws of this nature are those which forbid the wearing of arms, disarming those only who are not disposed to commit the crime which the laws mean to prevent. Can it be supposed that those who have the courage to violate the most sacred laws of humanity, and the most important of the code, will respect the less considerable and arbitrary injunctions, the violation of which is so easy, and of so little comparative importance? Does not the execution of this law deprive the subject of that personal liberty, so dear to mankind and to the wise legislator? And does it not subject the innocent to all the disagreeable circumstances that should only fall on the guilty? It certainly makes the situation of the assaulted worse, and of the assailants better, and rather encourages than prevents murder, as it requires less courage to attack unarmed than armed persons." —Cesare Beccaria

<u>September 11, 1997: Charlton Heston's Timeless Speech</u>
On September 11, 1997, Charlton Heston gave a timeless speech for the National Press Club (https://www.c-span.org/video/?c4716592/charlton-heston-bear-arms) called "Why We Have Guns." Butchered versions abound on the Internet, and the transcript provided by the National Press Club on its own website is incomplete—which is not surprising, since the modern press likes to censor Constitutional conservatives, rather than celebrate free expression for all. If the abridgment is unintentional, it is merely unfortunate and a shame; but, in any case, consulting the original video clip became essential in being able to report Heston's speech accurately.

There was one place on the Internet where the full speech could be accessed: C-Span (the link is provided above). Knowing the nature of the Internet, and how it morphs daily, it appeared to be of importance to take on the task of accurately transcribing Heston's speech in full, lest it eventually be lost down the Orwellian "memory hole" that gobbles up so much information not deemed "politically correct" by the censors now working for America's Big Data companies. Since there is a new generation in need of being taught the eternal truths expressed in Heston's speech, his offering is faithfully transcribed here, without additions or deletions to the text of the speech (except for the underlined subheadings dividing the speech into sections):

<u>The Essential Right</u>
"Today, I want to talk to you about guns: why we have them, why the Bill of Rights guarantees that we can have them, and why my right to have a gun is more important than your right to rail against it in the press.

"I believe every good journalist needs to know why the Second Amendment must be considered more essential than the First Amendment. This may be a bitter pill to swallow, but the right to keep and bear arms is not archaic. It's not an outdated, dusty idea some old dead white guys dreamed up in fear of the Redcoats. No. It's just as essential to liberty today as it was in 1776.

"These words may not play well at the Press Club, but it's still the gospel down at the corner bar and grill. And your efforts to undermine the Second Amendment—to deride it and denigrate it, to degrade it, to readily accept diluting it and eagerly promote redefining it—threaten not only the physical well-being of millions of Americans but also the core concept of individual liberty our Founding Fathers struggled to perfect and protect.

"So now you know what doubtless does not surprise you. I believe strongly in the right of every law-abiding citizen to keep and bear arms, for what I think are good reasons.

"The original amendments we refer to as the Bill of Rights contain ten of what the Constitutional framers termed unalienable rights. These rights are ranked in random order and are linked by their essential equality. The Bill of Rights came to us with blinders on it. It doesn't recognize color or class or wealth. It protects not just the rights of actors or editors or reporters, but extends even to those we love to hate. That's why the most heinous criminals have rights until they are convicted of a crime.

"The beauty of the Constitution can be found in the way it takes human nature into consideration. We are not a docile species capable of co-existing within a perfect society under everlasting benevolent rule.

"We are what we are: egotistical, corruptible, vengeful; sometimes even a bit power-mad. The Bill of Rights recognizes this and builds the barricades that need to be in place to protect the individual.

America's First Freedom
"You, of course, remain zealous in your belief that a free nation must have a free press and free speech to battle injustice, unmask corruption, and provide a voice for those in need of a fair and impartial forum.

"I agree—wholeheartedly—a free press is vital to a free society. But I wonder: How many of you will agree with me that the right to keep and bear arms is not just equally vital, but the most vital to protect all the other rights we enjoy?

"I say that the Second Amendment is, in order of importance, the first amendment. It is America's First Freedom, the one right that protects all the others. Among freedom of speech, of the press, of religion, of assembly, of redress of grievances, it is the first among equals. It alone offers the absolute capacity to live without fear. The right to keep and bear arms is the one right that allows 'rights' to exist at all.

"Now, either you believe that, or you don't, and you must decide. Because there is no such thing as a free nation where police and military are allowed the force of arms but individual citizens are not. That's a 'Big Brother knows best' theater of the absurd that has never boded well for the peasant class, the working class, or even for reporters.

"Yes, our Constitution provides the doorway for your news and commentary to pass through free and unfettered. But that doorway to freedom is framed by the muskets that stood between a vision of liberty and absolute anarchy at a place called Concord Bridge. Our Revolution began when the British sent Redcoats door to door to confiscate the people's guns. They didn't succeed; the muskets went out the back door with their owners.

"Emerson said it best:
'By the rude bridge that arched the flood,
Their flag to April's breeze unfurled,
Here once the embattled farmers stood,
And fired the shot heard round the world.'

"King George called us 'rabble-rousers, rabble in arms.' But with God's grace, George Washington and many brave men gave us our country. Soon after, God's grace and a few great men gave us our Constitution. It's been said that the creation of the United States is the greatest political act in history. I'll sign that.

Totalitarian Dictators & Gun Confiscation
"In the next two centuries, though, freedom did not flourish. The next Revolution, the French, collapsed in bloody Terror, followed by Napoleon's tyranny. There's been no shortage of dictators since, in many countries: Hitler, Mussolini, Stalin, Mao, Idi Amin, Castro, Pol Pot. All these monsters began by confiscating private arms, then literally soaking the earth with the blood of tens and tens of millions of their people. Ah, the joys of gun control!

"Now, I doubt any of you would prefer a rolled up newspaper as a weapon against a dictator or a criminal intruder. Yet, in essence, that is what you have asked our loved ones to do, through the ill-contrived and totally naïve campaign against the Second Amendment.

"Besides, how can we entrust to you the Second Amendment when you are so stingy with your own First Amendment? I say this because of the way, in recent days, you have treated your own—those journalists you consider the least among you. How quick you've been to finger the paparazzi with blame and to eye the tabloids with disdain. How eager you've been to draw a line where there is none, to demand some distinction within the First Amendment that sneers, 'They are not one of us!' How readily you let your lesser brethren take the fall, as if their rights were not as worthy, and their purpose not as pure, and their freedom not as sacred as yours!

"So now, as politicians consider new laws to shackle and gag paparazzi, who among you will speak out? Who here will stand and defend them? Well, if you won't, I will. Because you do not define the First Amendment; it defines you. And it is bigger than you. Big enough to embrace all of you, plus all of those you would exclude. That's how freedom works.

"It also demands you do your homework. Again and again, I hear gun owners say, 'How can we believe anything that anti-gun media says when they cannot even get the facts right?' For too long you've swallowed manufactured statistics and fabricated technical support from anti-gun organizations that wouldn't know a semi-auto from a sharp stick. And it shows. You fall for it every time.

"That's why you have very little credibility among 70 million gun owners and 20 million hunters and many millions of veterans who learned the hard way which end the bullet comes out. And while you attacked the amendment that defends your homes and protects your spouses and children, you have denied those of us who defend all the Bill of Rights a fair hearing or the courtesy of an honest debate.

"If the NRA attempts to challenge your assertions, we are ignored. And if we try to buy advertising time or space to answer your charges, more often than not we are denied. How's that for First Amendment freedom?

"Clearly, too many have used freedom of the press as a weapon—not only to strangle our free speech, but to erode and ultimately destroy the right to keep and bear arms as well. In doing so, you promoted your profession to that of Constitutional judge and jury, more powerful even than our Supreme Court, more prejudiced than the Inquisition's tribunals. It's a frightening misuse of Constitutional right, and I pray that you will come to your senses and see that these abuses are curbed.

"As a veteran of World War Two, as a freedom marcher who stood with Dr. Martin Luther King long before it was fashionable, and as a grandfather who wants the coming century to be free and full of promise for my grandchildren, I am troubled.

Freedom Under Threat
"The right to keep and bear arms is threatened by political theatrics, piecemeal lawmaking, talk-show psychology, extreme bad taste in the entertainment industry, an ever-widening educational chasm in our schools, and a conniving media that all add up to cultural warfare against the idea that guns ever had, or should now have, an honorable and proud place in our society.

"But all of our rights must be delivered into the 21st century as pure and complete as they came to us at the beginning of this century. Traditionally, the passing of that torch is from a gnarled old hand down to an eager young one. So now, at 72, I offer my gnarled old hand.

"I've accepted a call from the National Rifle Association of America to help protect the Second Amendment. I feel it is my duty to do that. My mission and vision can be summarized in three simple parts:

"First, before we enter the next century, I expect to see a pro-Second Amendment president in the White House.

"Secondly, I expect to build an NRA with the political muscle and clout to keep a pro-Second Amendment Congress in place.

"Third is a promise to the next generation of free Americans: I hope to help raise a hundred million dollars for NRA programs and education before the year 2000; at least half of that sum will go to teach American kids what the right to keep and bear arms really means to their culture and country.

"We've raised a generation of young people who think that the Bill of Rights comes with their cable TV. Leave them to their channel surfing and they'll remain oblivious to history and heritage that truly matter.

"Think about it: What else must young Americans think when the White House proclaims, as it did, that 'a firearm in the hands of youth is a crime or an accident waiting to happen'? No. It's time they learned that firearm ownership is Constitutional, not criminal. In fact, few pursuits can teach a young person more about responsibility, safety, conservation, their history, and their heritage all at once.

Misled by Politically-Correct Doctrine

"It's time they found out that the politically-correct doctrine of today has misled them, and that, when they reach legal age, if they do not break our laws, they have a right to choose to own a gun—a handgun, a long gun, a small gun, a large gun, a black gun, a purple gun, a pretty gun, an ugly gun—and to use that gun to defend themselves and their loved ones or to engage in any lawful purpose they desire without apology or explanation to anyone, ever.

"This is their first freedom. If you say it's outdated, then you haven't read your own headlines. If you say guns are destroying our society, I would answer that you know better. Declining morals, disintegrating families, vacillating political leadership, an eroding criminal justice system, and social mores that blur right and wrong are more to blame—certainly more than any legally owned firearm.

Rescuing Freedom

"I want to rescue the Second Amendment from an opportunistic president and from a press that apparently can't comprehend that attacks on the Second Amendment set the stage for assaults on the First.

"I want to save the Second Amendment from all these nitpicking little wars of attrition—fights over alleged Saturday-Night Specials, plastic guns, cop-killer bullets, and so many other made-for-prime-time non-issues invented by some press agent over at Gun Control Headquarters—that you guys buy time and again.

"I simply cannot stand and watch a right guaranteed by the Constitution of the United States come apart, under attack from those who either can't understand it, don't like the sound of it, or find themselves too philosophically squeamish to see why it remains the first among equals: Because it is the right we turn to when all else fails!

"That's why the Second Amendment is America's First Freedom.

"Please, go forth and tell the truth. There can be no free speech, no freedom of the press, no freedom to protest, no freedom to worship your god, no freedom to speak your mind, no freedom from fear, no freedom for your children and for theirs, for anybody, anywhere, without the Second Amendment freedom to fight for it.

"If you don't believe me, just turn on the news tonight. Civilization's veneer is wearing thinner all the time.

"Thank you."

Appendix F: The Bill of Rights' Forgotten Amendment—The Third

"Ultimately property rights and personal rights are the same thing." —Calvin Coolidge

<u>An Often Overlooked Civil Right</u>
The text of the Third Amendment to the US Constitution reads as follows: "No Soldier shall, in time of peace be quartered in any house, without the consent of the Owner, nor in time of war, but in a manner to be prescribed by law."

These words are important, but they are much overlooked and seldom thought about. It would seem the government has violated this fundamental Natural Right not to have one's private home invaded and appropriated for government use, without consent, on several occasions. A review of them, in light of this extreme governmental overreach, might be wise at this time.

<u>CASE #1: During the Obama Administration</u>
On July 10, 2011, the Henderson, Nevada, police paid the Mitchell family a call. They wanted to use the family home to investigate a neighbor. The police smashed in the door and forced Anthony Mitchell to the floor at gunpoint, shooting him and his dog with pepper-spray pellets. To add insult to injury, Mr. Mitchell was also arrested for "obstructing a police officer." That same day, the police also quartered themselves in the home of Anthony Mitchell's parents in the same neighborhood, charging his father with obstructing an officer, as well.

Although the police eventually dropped all charges against both families, all family members have signed on to the same 18-page legal complaint against the city. The city has argued that the police are not subject to the Third Amendment. But Frank Cofer, the family's lawyer, has issued a statement, wherein he has said, "I'm confident the Mitchells have a good case," making much of the fact that the officers made use of military-style tactics during the incident. "And, after entering their houses, they drank water, ate food, [and] enjoyed the air conditioning. That struck me as quartering."

<u>CASE #2: During the Carter Administration</u>
There was an important Third Amendment Case filed in 1979, which came to be known as *Engblom v. Carey*. It is the only legally significant court decision based on a direct civil rights challenge under the Third Amendment.

The case was initially brought to court by New York State correction officers in 1979, because, while they were on strike, many of their duties were performed by National Guardsmen. The striking employees were evicted from employee housing, so the National Guard could use it. Two of the evicted officers subsequently filed suit.

On May 3, 1982, the court found that National Guardsmen do legally qualify as soldiers under the Third Amendment. This would mean that the amendment applies to state as well as federal authorities, and that Third Amendment protection extends to renters as well as homeowners.

The case was then remanded to district court, where it was decided that the National Guardsmen were immune to suit as agents of the state, since they did not knowingly act in an illegal manner. Nevertheless, the higher court finding that National Guardsmen are the same as soldiers for the purposes of the Third Amendment is a major win for the American people.

<u>CASE #3: During the Roosevelt Administration</u>
During World War Two, as a result of a Japanese attack against the Aleutian Islands, the government forced residents to leave their homes to allow the quartering of troops.

The problem posed by this case is the meaning of "property" in the Constitution, where property is mentioned four times. The unjust treatment of Aleutian natives shows the risk of giving Constitutional property too narrow a definition.

The Supreme Court's reticence in taking up this issue may lie in the fact that there are inconsistencies that afflict the law of Constitutional property that would require the Court to come up with a consistent meaning that could easily be applied throughout the Constitution.

The Third Amendment does allow forcible quartering of troops in private homes during wartime "in a manner to be prescribed by law." But, since Congress has never enacted any such law, the fact that the government did this to the Aleuts becomes legally problematic.

It must be pointed out that the peripheral effects that arose as a result of this quartering were horrible for the Aleuts to endure. Beyond the quartering of the soldiers, their injuries consist of the following: 1) they were forcibly removed from their homes; 2) they were interred in camps; 3) many died in the unhealthy conditions, including most of the elders vital to sustaining their culture; 4) in order to deny the Japanese a useful base, a burnt-earth policy was followed, completely destroying several villages; 5) other empty villages were comprehensively ransacked by soldiers; 6) Aleuts were not allowed to go home for a year, at which time they found all their possessions to be missing; 7) stolen family mementos, heirlooms, and religious icons were never recovered. Thus, the quartering was not even the worst thing that happened, although it was the gateway incident that allowed all the other atrocities to occur.

It is true that the Aleuts were finally given partial compensation for their losses in the 1980s, but officials refused to admit that Aleuts had suffered a violation of their civil rights. The amount of compensation received by each survivor was only $12,000. The failure of the government to consider this a Constitutional violation indicates the lack of concern that government is all-too-prone to exhibit.

<u>Still Neglected</u>
It bears mentioning that, to this date, the Supreme Court has never directly addressed the

meaning of the Third Amendment. Perhaps the closest thing we can find to it is a mention of the amendment in *Griswold v. Connecticut* (1965), when the Court cited the Third Amendment as one part of the Bill of Rights that proves that there exist "zones of privacy" and a Constitutional right to privacy.

Perhaps it is time for the Supreme Court to take up the Third Amendment and make it clear that a soldier by any other name is still an unwelcome government intrusion into the private sphere of the American citizen.

Appendix G: The Constitution of the United States

We the People of the United States, in Order to form a more perfect Union, establish Justice, insure domestic Tranquility, provide for the common defence, promote the general Welfare, and secure the Blessings of Liberty to ourselves and our Posterity, do ordain and establish this Constitution for the United States of America.

Article. I.

Section. 1.

All legislative Powers herein granted shall be vested in a Congress of the United States, which shall consist of a Senate and House of Representatives.

Section. 2.

The House of Representatives shall be composed of Members chosen every second Year by the People of the several States, and the Electors in each State shall have the Qualifications requisite for Electors of the most numerous Branch of the State Legislature.

No Person shall be a Representative who shall not have attained to the Age of twenty five Years, and been seven Years a Citizen of the United States, and who shall not, when elected, be an Inhabitant of that State in which he shall be chosen.

Representatives and direct Taxes shall be apportioned among the several States which may be included within this Union, according to their respective Numbers, which shall be determined by adding to the whole Number of free Persons, including those bound to Service for a Term of Years, and excluding Indians not taxed, three fifths of all other Persons. The actual Enumeration shall be made within three Years after the first Meeting of the Congress of the United States, and within every subsequent Term of ten Years, in such Manner as they shall by Law direct. The Number of Representatives shall not exceed one for every thirty Thousand, but each State shall have at Least one Representative; and until such enumeration shall be made, the State of New Hampshire shall be entitled to chuse three, Massachusetts eight, Rhode-Island and Providence Plantations one, Connecticut five, New-York six, New Jersey four, Pennsylvania eight, Delaware one, Maryland six, Virginia ten, North Carolina five, South Carolina five, and Georgia three.

When vacancies happen in the Representation from any State, the Executive Authority thereof shall issue Writs of Election to fill such Vacancies.

The House of Representatives shall chuse their Speaker and other Officers; and shall have the sole Power of Impeachment.

Section. 3.

The Senate of the United States shall be composed of two Senators from each State, chosen by the Legislature thereof, for six Years; and each Senator shall have one Vote.

Immediately after they shall be assembled in Consequence of the first Election, they shall be divided as equally as may be into three Classes. The Seats of the Senators of the first Class shall be vacated at the Expiration of the second Year, of the second Class at the Expiration of the fourth Year, and of the third Class at the Expiration of the sixth Year, so that one third may be chosen every second Year; and if Vacancies happen by Resignation, or otherwise, during the Recess of the Legislature of any State, the Executive thereof may make temporary Appointments until the next Meeting of the Legislature, which shall then fill such Vacancies.

No Person shall be a Senator who shall not have attained to the Age of thirty Years, and been nine Years a Citizen of the United States, and who shall not, when elected, be an Inhabitant of that State for which he shall be chosen.

The Vice President of the United States shall be President of the Senate, but shall have no Vote, unless they be equally divided.

The Senate shall chuse their other Officers, and also a President pro tempore, in the Absence of the Vice President, or when he shall exercise the Office of President of the United States.

The Senate shall have the sole Power to try all Impeachments. When sitting for that Purpose, they shall be on Oath or Affirmation. When the President of the United States is tried, the Chief Justice shall preside: And no Person shall be convicted without the Concurrence of two thirds of the Members present.

Judgment in Cases of Impeachment shall not extend further than to removal from Office, and disqualification to hold and enjoy any Office of honor, Trust or Profit under the United States: but the Party convicted shall nevertheless be liable and subject to Indictment, Trial, Judgment and Punishment, according to Law.

Section. 4.

The Times, Places and Manner of holding Elections for Senators and Representatives, shall be prescribed in each State by the Legislature thereof; but the Congress may at any time by Law make or alter such Regulations, except as to the Places of chusing Senators.

The Congress shall assemble at least once in every Year, and such Meeting shall be on the first Monday in December, unless they shall by Law appoint a different Day.

Section. 5.

Each House shall be the Judge of the Elections, Returns and Qualifications of its own Members, and a Majority of each shall constitute a Quorum to do Business; but a smaller Number may adjourn from day to day, and may be authorized to compel the Attendance of absent Members, in such Manner, and under such Penalties as each House may provide.

Each House may determine the Rules of its Proceedings, punish its Members for disorderly Behaviour, and, with the Concurrence of two thirds, expel a Member.

Each House shall keep a Journal of its Proceedings, and from time to time publish the same, excepting such Parts as may in their Judgment require Secrecy; and the Yeas and Nays of the Members of either House on any question shall, at the Desire of one fifth of those Present, be entered on the Journal.

Neither House, during the Session of Congress, shall, without the Consent of the other, adjourn for more than three days, nor to any other Place than that in which the two Houses shall be sitting.

Section. 6.

The Senators and Representatives shall receive a Compensation for their Services, to be ascertained by Law, and paid out of the Treasury of the United States. They shall in all Cases, except Treason, Felony and Breach of the Peace, be privileged from Arrest during their Attendance at the Session of their respective Houses, and in going to and returning from the same; and for any Speech or Debate in either House, they shall not be questioned in any other Place.

No Senator or Representative shall, during the Time for which he was elected, be appointed to any civil Office under the Authority of the United States, which shall have been created, or the Emoluments whereof shall have been encreased during such time; and no Person holding any Office under the United States, shall be a Member of either House during his Continuance in Office.

Section. 7.

All Bills for raising Revenue shall originate in the House of Representatives; but the Senate may propose or concur with Amendments as on other Bills.

Every Bill which shall have passed the House of Representatives and the Senate, shall, before it become a Law, be presented to the President of the United States; If he approve he shall sign it, but if not he shall return it, with his Objections to that House in which it shall have originated, who shall enter the Objections at large on their Journal, and proceed to reconsider it. If after such Reconsideration two thirds of that House shall agree to pass the Bill, it shall be sent, together with the Objections, to the other House, by which it shall likewise be reconsidered, and if approved by two thirds of that House, it shall become a Law. But in all such Cases the Votes of both Houses shall be determined by yeas and Nays, and the Names of the Persons voting for and against the Bill shall be entered on the Journal of each House respectively. If any Bill shall not be returned by the President within ten Days (Sundays excepted) after it shall have been presented to him, the Same shall be a Law, in like Manner as if he had signed it, unless the Congress by their Adjournment prevent its Return, in which Case it shall not be a Law.

Every Order, Resolution, or Vote to which the Concurrence of the Senate and House of Representatives may be necessary (except on a question of Adjournment) shall be presented to the President of the United States; and before the Same shall take Effect, shall be approved by him, or being disapproved by him, shall be repassed by two thirds of the Senate and House of Representatives, according to the Rules and Limitations prescribed in the Case of a Bill.

Section. 8.

The Congress shall have Power To lay and collect Taxes, Duties, Imposts and Excises, to pay the Debts and provide for the common Defence and general Welfare of the United States; but all Duties, Imposts and Excises shall be uniform throughout the United States;

To borrow Money on the credit of the United States;

To regulate Commerce with foreign Nations, and among the several States, and with the Indian Tribes;

To establish an uniform Rule of Naturalization, and uniform Laws on the subject of Bankruptcies throughout the United States;

To coin Money, regulate the Value thereof, and of foreign Coin, and fix the Standard of Weights and Measures;

To provide for the Punishment of counterfeiting the Securities and current Coin of the United States;

To establish Post Offices and post Roads;

To promote the Progress of Science and useful Arts, by securing for limited Times to Authors and Inventors the exclusive Right to their respective Writings and Discoveries;

To constitute Tribunals inferior to the supreme Court;

To define and punish Piracies and Felonies committed on the high Seas, and Offences against the Law of Nations;

To declare War, grant Letters of Marque and Reprisal, and make Rules concerning Captures on Land and Water;

To raise and support Armies, but no Appropriation of Money to that Use shall be for a longer Term than two Years;

To provide and maintain a Navy;

To make Rules for the Government and Regulation of the land and naval Forces;

To provide for calling forth the Militia to execute the Laws of the Union, suppress Insurrections and repel Invasions;

To provide for organizing, arming, and disciplining, the Militia, and for governing such Part of them as may be employed in the Service of the United States, reserving to the States respectively, the Appointment of the Officers, and the Authority of training the Militia according to the discipline prescribed by Congress;

To exercise exclusive Legislation in all Cases whatsoever, over such District (not exceeding ten Miles square) as may, by Cession of particular States, and the Acceptance of Congress, become the Seat of the Government of the United States, and to exercise like Authority over all Places purchased by the Consent of the Legislature of the State in which the Same shall be, for the Erection of Forts, Magazines, Arsenals, dock-Yards, and other needful Buildings;—And

To make all Laws which shall be necessary and proper for carrying into Execution the foregoing Powers, and all other Powers vested by this Constitution in the Government of the United States, or in any Department or Officer thereof.

Section. 9.

The Migration or Importation of such Persons as any of the States now existing shall think proper to admit, shall not be prohibited by the Congress prior to the Year one thousand eight hundred and eight, but a Tax or duty may be imposed on such Importation, not exceeding ten dollars for each Person.

The Privilege of the Writ of Habeas Corpus shall not be suspended, unless when in Cases of Rebellion or Invasion the public Safety may require it.

No Bill of Attainder or ex post facto Law shall be passed.

No Capitation, or other direct, Tax shall be laid, unless in Proportion to the Census or enumeration herein before directed to be taken.

No Tax or Duty shall be laid on Articles exported from any State.

No Preference shall be given by any Regulation of Commerce or Revenue to the Ports of one State over those of another: nor shall Vessels bound to, or from, one State, be obliged to enter, clear, or pay Duties in another.

No Money shall be drawn from the Treasury, but in Consequence of Appropriations made by Law; and a regular Statement and Account of the Receipts and Expenditures of all public Money shall be published from time to time.

No Title of Nobility shall be granted by the United States: And no Person holding any Office of Profit or Trust under them, shall, without the Consent of the Congress, accept of any present, Emolument, Office, or Title, of any kind whatever, from any King, Prince, or foreign State.

Section. 10.

No State shall enter into any Treaty, Alliance, or Confederation; grant Letters of Marque and Reprisal; coin Money; emit Bills of Credit; make any Thing but gold and silver Coin a Tender in Payment of Debts; pass any Bill of Attainder, ex post facto Law, or Law impairing the Obligation of Contracts, or grant any Title of Nobility.

No State shall, without the Consent of the Congress, lay any Imposts or Duties on Imports or Exports, except what may be absolutely necessary for executing its inspection Laws: and the net Produce of all Duties and Imposts, laid by any State on Imports or Exports, shall be for the Use of the Treasury of the United States; and all such Laws shall be subject to the Revision and Controul of the Congress.

No State shall, without the Consent of Congress, lay any Duty of Tonnage, keep Troops, or Ships of War in time of Peace, enter into any Agreement or Compact with another State, or with a foreign Power, or engage in War, unless actually invaded, or in such imminent Danger as will not admit of delay.

Article. II.

Section. 1.

The executive Power shall be vested in a President of the United States of America. He shall hold his Office during the Term of four Years, and, together with the Vice President, chosen for the same Term, be elected, as follows

Each State shall appoint, in such Manner as the Legislature thereof may direct, a Number of Electors, equal to the whole Number of Senators and Representatives to which the State may be entitled in the Congress: but no Senator or Representative, or Person holding an Office of Trust or Profit under the United States, shall be appointed an Elector.

The Electors shall meet in their respective States, and vote by Ballot for two Persons, of whom one at least shall not be an Inhabitant of the same State with themselves. And they shall make a List of all the Persons voted for, and of the Number of Votes for each; which List they shall sign and certify, and transmit sealed to the Seat of the Government of the United States, directed to the President of the Senate. The President of the Senate shall, in the Presence of the Senate and House of Representatives, open all the Certificates, and the Votes shall then be counted. The Person having the greatest Number of Votes shall be the President, if such Number be a Majority of the whole Number of Electors appointed; and if there be more than one who have such Majority, and have an equal Number of Votes, then the House of Representatives shall immediately chuse by Ballot one of them for President; and if no Person have a Majority, then from the five highest on the List the said House shall in like Manner chuse the President. But in chusing the President, the Votes shall be taken by States, the Representation from each State having one Vote; A quorum for this Purpose shall consist of a Member or Members from two thirds of the States, and a Majority of all the States shall be necessary to a Choice. In every Case, after the Choice of the President, the Person having the greatest Number of Votes of the Electors shall be the Vice President. But if there should remain two or more who have equal Votes, the Senate shall chuse from them by Ballot the Vice President.

The Congress may determine the Time of chusing the Electors, and the Day on which they shall give their Votes; which Day shall be the same throughout the United States.

No Person except a natural born Citizen, or a Citizen of the United States, at the time of the Adoption of this Constitution, shall be eligible to the Office of President; neither shall any Person be eligible to that Office who shall not have attained to the Age of thirty five Years, and been fourteen Years a Resident within the United States.

In Case of the Removal of the President from Office, or of his Death, Resignation, or Inability to discharge the Powers and Duties of the said Office, the Same shall devolve on the Vice President, and the Congress may by Law provide for the Case of Removal, Death, Resignation or Inability, both of the President and Vice President, declaring what Officer shall then act as President, and such Officer shall act accordingly, until the Disability be removed, or a President shall be elected.

The President shall, at stated Times, receive for his Services, a Compensation, which shall neither be encreased nor diminished during the Period for which he shall have been elected, and he shall not receive within that Period any other Emolument from the United States, or any of them.

Before he enter on the Execution of his Office, he shall take the following Oath or Affirmation:—"I do solemnly swear (or affirm) that I will faithfully execute the Office of President of the United States, and will to the best of my Ability, preserve, protect and defend the Constitution of the United States."

Section. 2.

The President shall be Commander in Chief of the Army and Navy of the United States, and of the Militia of the several States, when called into the actual Service of the United States; he may require the Opinion, in writing, of the principal Officer in each of the executive Departments, upon any Subject relating to the Duties of their respective Offices, and he shall have Power to grant Reprieves and Pardons for Offences against the United States, except in Cases of Impeachment.

He shall have Power, by and with the Advice and Consent of the Senate, to make Treaties, provided two thirds of the Senators present concur; and he shall nominate, and by and with the Advice and Consent of the Senate, shall appoint Ambassadors, other public Ministers and Consuls, Judges of the supreme Court, and all other Officers of the United States, whose Appointments are not herein otherwise provided for, and which shall be established by Law: but the Congress may by Law vest the Appointment of such inferior Officers, as they think proper, in the President alone, in the Courts of Law, or in the Heads of Departments.

The President shall have Power to fill up all Vacancies that may happen during the Recess of the Senate, by granting Commissions which shall expire at the End of their next Session.

Section. 3.

He shall from time to time give to the Congress Information of the State of the Union, and recommend to their Consideration such Measures as he shall judge necessary and expedient; he may, on extraordinary Occasions, convene both Houses, or either of them, and in Case of Disagreement between them, with Respect to the Time of Adjournment, he may adjourn them to such Time as he shall think proper; he shall receive Ambassadors and other public Ministers; he shall take Care that the Laws be faithfully executed, and shall Commission all the Officers of the United States.

Section. 4.

The President, Vice President and all civil Officers of the United States, shall be removed from Office on Impeachment for, and Conviction of, Treason, Bribery, or other high Crimes and Misdemeanors.

Article III.

Section. 1.

The judicial Power of the United States, shall be vested in one supreme Court, and in such inferior Courts as the Congress may from time to time ordain and establish. The Judges, both of the supreme and inferior Courts, shall hold their Offices during good Behaviour, and shall, at stated Times, receive for their Services, a Compensation, which shall not be diminished during their Continuance in Office.

Section. 2.

The judicial Power shall extend to all Cases, in Law and Equity, arising under this Constitution, the Laws of the United States, and Treaties made, or which shall be made, under their Authority;—to all Cases affecting Ambassadors, other public Ministers and Consuls;—to all Cases of admiralty and maritime Jurisdiction;—to Controversies to which the United States shall be a Party;—to Controversies between two or more States;— between a State and Citizens of another State,—between Citizens of different States,—between Citizens of the same State claiming Lands under Grants of different States, and between a State, or the Citizens thereof, and foreign States, Citizens or Subjects.

In all Cases affecting Ambassadors, other public Ministers and Consuls, and those in which a State shall be Party, the supreme Court shall have original Jurisdiction. In all the other Cases before mentioned, the supreme Court shall have appellate Jurisdiction, both as to Law and Fact, with such Exceptions, and under such Regulations as the Congress shall make.

The Trial of all Crimes, except in Cases of Impeachment, shall be by Jury; and such Trial shall be held in the State where the said Crimes shall have been committed; but when not committed within any State, the Trial shall be at such Place or Places as the Congress may by Law have directed.

Section. 3.

Treason against the United States, shall consist only in levying War against them, or in adhering to their Enemies, giving them Aid and Comfort. No Person shall be convicted of Treason unless on the Testimony of two Witnesses to the same overt Act, or on Confession in open Court.

The Congress shall have Power to declare the Punishment of Treason, but no Attainder of Treason shall work Corruption of Blood, or Forfeiture except during the Life of the Person attainted.

Article. IV.

Section. 1.

Full Faith and Credit shall be given in each State to the public Acts, Records, and judicial Proceedings of every other State. And the Congress may by general Laws prescribe the Manner in which such Acts, Records and Proceedings shall be proved, and the Effect thereof.

Section. 2.

The Citizens of each State shall be entitled to all Privileges and Immunities of Citizens in the several States.

A Person charged in any State with Treason, Felony, or other Crime, who shall flee from Justice, and be found in another State, shall on Demand of the executive Authority of the State from which he fled, be delivered up, to be removed to the State having Jurisdiction of the Crime.

No Person held to Service or Labour in one State, under the Laws thereof, escaping into another, shall, in Consequence of any Law or Regulation therein, be discharged from such Service or Labour, but shall be delivered up on Claim of the Party to whom such Service or Labour may be due.

Section. 3.

New States may be admitted by the Congress into this Union; but no new State shall be formed or erected within the Jurisdiction of any other State; nor any State be formed by the Junction of two or more States, or Parts of States, without the Consent of the Legislatures of the States concerned as well as of the Congress.

The Congress shall have Power to dispose of and make all needful Rules and Regulations respecting the Territory or other Property belonging to the United States; and nothing in this Constitution shall be so construed as to Prejudice any Claims of the United States, or of any particular State.

Section. 4.

The United States shall guarantee to every State in this Union a Republican Form of Government, and shall protect each of them against Invasion; and on Application of the Legislature, or of the Executive (when the Legislature cannot be convened), against domestic Violence.

Article. V.

The Congress, whenever two thirds of both Houses shall deem it necessary, shall propose Amendments to this Constitution, or, on the Application of the Legislatures of two thirds of the several States, shall call a Convention for proposing Amendments, which, in either Case, shall be valid to all Intents and Purposes, as Part of this Constitution, when ratified by the Legislatures of three fourths of the several States, or by Conventions in three fourths thereof, as the one or the other Mode of Ratification may be proposed by the Congress; Provided that no Amendment which may be made prior to the Year One thousand eight hundred and eight shall in any Manner affect the first and fourth Clauses in the Ninth Section of the first Article; and that no State, without its Consent, shall be deprived of its equal Suffrage in the Senate.

Article. VI.

All Debts contracted and Engagements entered into, before the Adoption of this Constitution, shall be as valid against the United States under this Constitution, as under the Confederation.

This Constitution, and the Laws of the United States which shall be made in Pursuance thereof; and all Treaties made, or which shall be made, under the Authority of the United States, shall be the supreme Law of the Land; and the Judges in every State shall be bound thereby, any Thing in the Constitution or Laws of any State to the Contrary notwithstanding.

The Senators and Representatives before mentioned, and the Members of the several State Legislatures, and all executive and judicial Officers, both of the United States and of the several States, shall be bound by Oath or Affirmation, to support this Constitution; but no religious Test shall ever be required as a Qualification to any Office or public Trust under the United States.

Article. VII.

The Ratification of the Conventions of nine States, shall be sufficient for the Establishment of this Constitution between the States so ratifying the Same.

Attest William Jackson Secretary

done in Convention by the Unanimous Consent of the States present the Seventeenth Day of September in the Year of our Lord one thousand seven hundred and Eighty seven and of the Independance of the United States of America the Twelfth In witness whereof We have hereunto subscribed our Names,

G°. Washington
Presidt and deputy from Virginia

Delaware

Geo: Read

Gunning Bedford jun

John Dickinson

Richard Bassett

Jaco: Broom

Maryland

James McHenry

Dan of St Thos. Jenifer

Danl. Carroll

Virginia

John Blair

James Madison Jr.

North Carolina

Wm. Blount

Richd. Dobbs Spaight

Hu Williamson

South Carolina

J. Rutledge

Charles Cotesworth Pinckney

Charles Pinckney

Pierce Butler

Georgia

William Few

Abr Baldwin

New Hampshire

John Langdon

Nicholas Gilman

Massachusetts

Nathaniel Gorham

Rufus King

Connecticut

Wm. Saml. Johnson

Roger Sherman

New York

Alexander Hamilton

New Jersey

Wil: Livingston

David Brearley

Wm. Paterson

Jona: Dayton

Pennsylvania

B Franklin

Thomas Mifflin

Robt. Morris

Geo. Clymer

Thos. FitzSimons

Jared Ingersoll

James Wilson

Gouv Morris

[Rhode Island

No delegates from Rhode Island were in attendance.]

Appendix H: The US Constitution, Amendments 1-10, The Bill of Rights

[The following text is a transcription of the first ten amendments in their original form, as submitted to the states. This "Bill of Rights" was ratified on December 15, 1791.]

The Preamble to The Bill of Rights

Congress of the United States
begun and held at the City of New-York, on
Wednesday the fourth of March, one thousand seven hundred and eighty nine.

THE Conventions of a number of the States, having at the time of their adopting the Constitution, expressed a desire, in order to prevent misconstruction or abuse of its powers, that further declaratory and restrictive clauses should be added: And as extending the ground of public confidence in the Government, will best ensure the beneficent ends of its institution.

RESOLVED by the Senate and House of Representatives of the United States of America, in Congress assembled, two thirds of both Houses concurring, that the following Articles be proposed to the Legislatures of the several States, as amendments to the Constitution of the United States, all, or any of which Articles, when ratified by three fourths of the said Legislatures, to be valid to all intents and purposes, as part of the said Constitution; viz.

ARTICLES in addition to, and Amendment of the Constitution of the United States of America, proposed by Congress, and ratified by the Legislatures of the several States, pursuant to the fifth Article of the original Constitution.

AMENDMENT I

Congress shall make no law respecting an establishment of religion, or prohibiting the free exercise thereof; or abridging the freedom of speech, or of the press; or the right of the people peaceably to assemble, and to petition the Government for a redress of grievances.

AMENDMENT II

A well regulated Militia, being necessary to the security of a free State, the right of the people to keep and bear Arms, shall not be infringed.

AMENDMENT III

No Soldier shall, in time of peace be quartered in any house, without the consent of the Owner, nor in time of war, but in a manner to be prescribed by law.

AMENDMENT IV

The right of the people to be secure in their persons, houses, papers, and effects, against unreasonable searches and seizures, shall not be violated, and no Warrants shall issue, but upon probable cause, supported by Oath or affirmation, and particularly describing the place to be searched, and the persons or things to be seized.

AMENDMENT V

No person shall be held to answer for a capital, or otherwise infamous crime, unless on a presentment or indictment of a Grand Jury, except in cases arising in the land or naval forces, or in the Militia, when in actual service in time of War or public danger; nor shall any person be subject for the same offence to be twice put in jeopardy of life or limb; nor shall be compelled in any criminal case to be a witness against himself, nor be deprived of life, liberty, or property, without due process of law; nor shall private property be taken for public use, without just compensation.

AMENDMENT VI

In all criminal prosecutions, the accused shall enjoy the right to a speedy and public trial, by an impartial jury of the State and district wherein the crime shall have been committed, which district shall have been previously ascertained by law, and to be informed of the nature and cause of the accusation; to be confronted with the witnesses against him; to have compulsory process for obtaining witnesses in his favor, and to have the Assistance of Counsel for his defence.

AMENDMENT VII

In Suits at common law, where the value in controversy shall exceed twenty dollars, the right of trial by jury shall be preserved, and no fact tried by a jury, shall be otherwise re-examined in any Court of the United States, than according to the rules of the common law.

AMENDMENT VIII

Excessive bail shall not be required, nor excessive fines imposed, nor cruel and unusual punishments inflicted.

AMENDMENT IX

The enumeration in the Constitution, of certain rights, shall not be construed to deny or disparage others retained by the people.

AMENDMENT X

The powers not delegated to the United States by the Constitution, nor prohibited by it to the States, are reserved to the States respectively, or to the people.

Appendix I: The US Constitution, Amendments 11-27

[Amendments 1-10 make up the Bill of Rights. Amendments 11-27 follow.]

AMENDMENT XI

[Passed by Congress on March 4, 1794. Ratified on February 7, 1795. Note: Article III, Section 2, of the Constitution was modified by the 11th Amendment.]

The Judicial power of the United States shall not be construed to extend to any suit in law or equity, commenced or prosecuted against one of the United States by Citizens of another State, or by Citizens or Subjects of any Foreign State.

AMENDMENT XII

[Passed by Congress on December 9, 1803. Ratified on June 15, 1804. Note: A portion of Article II, Section 1, of the Constitution was superseded by the 12th Amendment.]

The Electors shall meet in their respective states and vote by ballot for President and Vice-President, one of whom, at least, shall not be an inhabitant of the same state with themselves; they shall name in their ballots the person voted for as President, and in distinct ballots the person voted for as Vice-President, and they shall make distinct lists of all persons voted for as President, and of all persons voted for as Vice-President, and of the number of votes for each, which lists they shall sign and certify, and transmit sealed to the seat of the government of the United States, directed to the President of the Senate;—the President of the Senate shall, in the presence of the Senate and House of Representatives, open all the certificates and the votes shall then be counted; —The person having the greatest number of votes for President, shall be the President, if such number be a majority of the whole number of Electors appointed; and if no person have such majority, then from the persons having the highest numbers not exceeding three on the list of those voted for as President, the House of Representatives shall choose immediately, by ballot, the President. But in choosing the President, the votes shall be taken by states, the representation from each state having one vote; a quorum for this purpose shall consist of a member or members from two-thirds of the states, and a majority of all the states shall be necessary to a choice. And if the House of Representatives shall not choose a President whenever the right of choice shall devolve upon them, before the fourth day of March next following, then the Vice-President shall act as President, as in case of the death or other constitutional disability of the President*.—The person having the greatest number of votes as Vice-President, shall be the Vice-President, if such number be a majority of the whole number of Electors appointed, and if no person have a majority, then from the two highest numbers on the list, the Senate shall choose the Vice-President; a quorum for the purpose shall consist of two-thirds of the whole number of Senators, and a majority of the whole number shall be necessary to a choice. But no person constitutionally ineligible to the office of President shall be eligible to that of Vice-President of the United States.

[*Superseded by Section 3 of the 20th amendment.]

AMENDMENT XIII

[Passed by Congress on January 31, 1865. Ratified on December 6, 1865. Note: A portion of Article IV, Section 2, of the Constitution was superseded by the 13th Amendment.]

Section 1.

Neither slavery nor involuntary servitude, except as a punishment for crime whereof the party shall have been duly convicted, shall exist within the United States, or any place subject to their jurisdiction.

Section 2.

Congress shall have power to enforce this article by appropriate legislation.

AMENDMENT XIV

[Passed by Congress on June 13, 1866. Ratified on July 9, 1868. Note: Article I, Section 2, of the Constitution was modified by Section 2 of the 14th amendment.]

Section 1.

All persons born or naturalized in the United States, and subject to the jurisdiction thereof, are citizens of the United States and of the State wherein they reside. No State shall make or enforce any law which shall abridge the privileges or immunities of citizens of the United States; nor shall any State deprive any person of life, liberty, or property, without due process of law; nor deny to any person within its jurisdiction the equal protection of the laws.

Section 2.

Representatives shall be apportioned among the several States according to their respective numbers, counting the whole number of persons in each State, excluding Indians not taxed. But when the right to vote at any election for the choice of electors for President and Vice-President of the United States, Representatives in Congress, the Executive and Judicial officers of a State, or the members of the Legislature thereof, is denied to any of the male inhabitants of such State, being twenty-one years of age*, and citizens of the United States, or in any way abridged, except for participation in rebellion, or other crime, the basis of representation therein shall be reduced in the proportion which the number of such male citizens shall bear to the whole number of male citizens twenty-one years of age in such State.

Section 3.

No person shall be a Senator or Representative in Congress, or elector of President and Vice-President, or hold any office, civil or military, under the United States, or under any State, who, having previously taken an oath, as a member of Congress, or as an officer of the United States, or as a member of any State legislature, or as an executive or judicial officer of any State, to support the Constitution of the United States, shall have engaged in insurrection or rebellion against the same, or given aid or comfort to the enemies thereof. But Congress may by a vote of two-thirds of each House, remove such disability.

Section 4.

The validity of the public debt of the United States, authorized by law, including debts incurred for payment of pensions and bounties for services in suppressing insurrection or rebellion, shall not be questioned. But neither the United States nor any State shall assume or pay any debt or obligation incurred in aid of insurrection or rebellion against the United States, or any claim for the loss or emancipation of any slave; but all such debts, obligations and claims shall be held illegal and void.

Section 5.

The Congress shall have the power to enforce, by appropriate legislation, the provisions of this article.

[*Changed by Section 1 of the 26th Amendment.]

AMENDMENT XV

[Passed by Congress on February 26, 1869. Ratified on February 3, 1870.]

Section 1.

The right of citizens of the United States to vote shall not be denied or abridged by the United States or by any State on account of race, color, or previous condition of servitude—

Section 2.

The Congress shall have the power to enforce this article by appropriate legislation.

AMENDMENT XVI

[Passed by Congress on July 2, 1909. Ratified on February 3, 1913. Note: Article I, Section 9, of the Constitution was modified by the 16th Amendment.]

The Congress shall have power to lay and collect taxes on incomes, from whatever source derived, without apportionment among the several States, and without regard to any census or enumeration.

AMENDMENT XVII

[Passed by Congress on May 13, 1912. Ratified on April 8, 1913. Note: Article I, Section 3, of the Constitution was modified by the 17th Amendment.]

The Senate of the United States shall be composed of two Senators from each State, elected by the people thereof, for six years; and each Senator shall have one vote. The electors in each State shall have the qualifications requisite for electors of the most numerous branch of the State legislatures.

When vacancies happen in the representation of any State in the Senate, the executive authority of such State shall issue writs of election to fill such vacancies: Provided, That the legislature of any State may empower the executive thereof to make temporary appointments until the people fill the vacancies by election as the legislature may direct.

This amendment shall not be so construed as to affect the election or term of any Senator chosen before it becomes valid as part of the Constitution.

AMENDMENT XVIII

[Passed by Congress on December 18, 1917. Ratified on January 16, 1919. Repealed by the 21st Amendment.]

Section 1.

After one year from the ratification of this article the manufacture, sale, or transportation of intoxicating liquors within, the importation thereof into, or the exportation thereof from the United States and all territory subject to the jurisdiction thereof for beverage purposes is hereby prohibited.

Section 2.

The Congress and the several States shall have concurrent power to enforce this article by appropriate legislation.

Section 3.

This article shall be inoperative unless it shall have been ratified as an amendment to the Constitution by the legislatures of the several States, as provided in the Constitution, within seven years from the date of the submission hereof to the States by the Congress.

AMENDMENT XIX

[Passed by Congress on June 4, 1919. Ratified on August 18, 1920.]

The right of citizens of the United States to vote shall not be denied or abridged by the United States or by any State on account of sex.

Congress shall have power to enforce this article by appropriate legislation.

AMENDMENT XX

[Passed by Congress on March 2, 1932. Ratified on January 23, 1933. Note: Article I, Section 4, of the Constitution was modified by Section 2 of this amendment. In addition, a portion of the 12th Amendment was superseded by section 3.]

Section 1.

The terms of the President and the Vice President shall end at noon on the 20th day of January, and the terms of Senators and Representatives at noon on the 3d day of January, of the years in which such terms would have ended if this article had not been ratified; and the terms of their successors shall then begin.

Section 2.
The Congress shall assemble at least once in every year, and such meeting shall begin at noon on the 3d day of January, unless they shall by law appoint a different day.

Section 3.
If, at the time fixed for the beginning of the term of the President, the President elect shall have died, the Vice President elect shall become President. If a President shall not have been chosen before the time fixed for the beginning of his term, or if the President elect shall have failed to qualify, then the Vice President elect shall act as President until a President shall have qualified; and the Congress may by law provide for the case wherein neither a President elect nor a Vice President elect shall have qualified, declaring who shall then act as President, or the manner in which one who is to act shall be selected, and such person shall act accordingly until a President or Vice President shall have qualified.

Section 4.

The Congress may by law provide for the case of the death of any of the persons from whom the House of Representatives may choose a President whenever the right of choice shall have devolved upon them, and for the case of the death of any of the persons from whom the Senate may choose a Vice President whenever the right of choice shall have devolved upon them.

Section 5.

Sections 1 and 2 shall take effect on the 15th day of October following the ratification of this article.

Section 6.

This article shall be inoperative unless it shall have been ratified as an amendment to the Constitution by the legislatures of three-fourths of the several States within seven years from the date of its submission.

AMENDMENT XXI

[Passed by Congress on February 20, 1933. Ratified on December 5, 1933.]

Section 1.

The eighteenth article of amendment to the Constitution of the United States is hereby repealed.

Section 2.

The transportation or importation into any State, Territory, or possession of the United States for delivery or use therein of intoxicating liquors, in violation of the laws thereof, is hereby prohibited.

Section 3.

This article shall be inoperative unless it shall have been ratified as an amendment to the Constitution by conventions in the several States, as provided in the Constitution, within seven years from the date of the submission hereof to the States by the Congress.

AMENDMENT XXII

[Passed by Congress on March 21, 1947. Ratified on February 27, 1951.]

Section 1.

No person shall be elected to the office of the President more than twice, and no person who has held the office of President, or acted as President, for more than two years of a term to which some other person was elected President shall be elected to the office of the President more than once. But this Article shall not apply to any person holding the office of President when this Article was proposed by the Congress, and shall not prevent any person who may be holding the office of President, or acting as President, during the term within which this Article becomes operative from holding the office of President or acting as President during the remainder of such term.

Section 2.

This article shall be inoperative unless it shall have been ratified as an amendment to the Constitution by the legislatures of three-fourths of the several States within seven years from the date of its submission to the States by the Congress.

AMENDMENT XXIII

[Passed by Congress June 16, 1960. Ratified March 29, 1961.]

Section 1.

The District constituting the seat of Government of the United States shall appoint in such manner as the Congress may direct:

A number of electors of President and Vice President equal to the whole number of Senators and Representatives in Congress to which the District would be entitled if it were a State, but in no event more than the least populous State; they shall be in addition to those appointed by the States, but they shall be considered, for the purposes of the election of President and Vice President, to be electors appointed by a State; and they shall meet in the District and perform such duties as provided by the twelfth article of amendment.

Section 2.

The Congress shall have power to enforce this article by appropriate legislation.

AMENDMENT XXIV

[Passed by Congress on August 27, 1962. Ratified on January 23, 1964.]
Section 1.

The right of citizens of the United States to vote in any primary or other election for President or

Vice President, for electors for President or Vice President, or for Senator or Representative in Congress, shall not be denied or abridged by the United States or any State by reason of failure to pay any poll tax or other tax.

Section 2.

The Congress shall have power to enforce this article by appropriate legislation.

AMENDMENT XXV

[Passed by Congress on July 6, 1965. Ratified on February 10, 1967. Note: Article II, Section 1, of the Constitution was affected by the 25th Amendment.]

Section 1.

In case of the removal of the President from office or of his death or resignation, the Vice President shall become President.

Section 2.

Whenever there is a vacancy in the office of the Vice President, the President shall nominate a Vice President who shall take office upon confirmation by a majority vote of both Houses of Congress.

Section 3.

Whenever the President transmits to the President pro tempore of the Senate and the Speaker of the House of Representatives his written declaration that he is unable to discharge the powers and duties of his office, and until he transmits to them a written declaration to the contrary, such powers and duties shall be discharged by the Vice President as Acting President.

Section 4.

Whenever the Vice President and a majority of either the principal officers of the executive departments or of such other body as Congress may by law provide, transmit to the President pro tempore of the Senate and the Speaker of the House of Representatives their written declaration that the President is unable to discharge the powers and duties of his office, the Vice President shall immediately assume the powers and duties of the office as Acting President.

Thereafter, when the President transmits to the President pro tempore of the Senate and the Speaker of the House of Representatives his written declaration that no inability exists, he shall resume the powers and duties of his office unless the Vice President and a majority of either the principal officers of the executive department or of such other body as Congress may by law provide, transmit within four days to the President pro tempore of the Senate and the Speaker of the House of Representatives their written declaration that the President is unable to discharge the powers and duties of his office. Thereupon Congress shall decide the issue, assembling within forty-eight hours for that purpose if not in session. If the Congress, within twenty-one days after receipt of the latter written declaration, or, if Congress is not in session, within twenty-one days after Congress is required to assemble, determines by two-thirds vote of both Houses that the President is unable to discharge the powers and duties of his office, the Vice President shall continue to discharge the same as Acting President; otherwise, the President shall resume the powers and duties of his office.

AMENDMENT XXVI

[Passed by Congress on March 23, 1971. Ratified on July 1, 1971. Note: Amendment 14, Section 2, of the Constitution was modified by Section 1 of the 26th amendment.]

Section 1.

The right of citizens of the United States, who are eighteen years of age or older, to vote shall not be denied or abridged by the United States or by any State on account of age.

Section 2.

The Congress shall have power to enforce this article by appropriate legislation.

AMENDMENT XXVII

[Originally proposed on Sept. 25, 1789. Ratified on May 7, 1992.]

No law, varying the compensation for the services of the Senators and Representatives, shall take effect, until an election of Representatives shall have intervened.

———

The Constitution transcribed in these appendices (G, H, and I) follows the inscription of Jacob Shallus' original on parchment, which is on display in the Rotunda of the National Archives Museum: https://www.archives.gov/founding-docs/constitution-transcript. The spelling and punctuation are consistent with that document.

Appendix J: A First Principles Primer: The Biblical Foundation of the US Constitution

"God, who gave us life, gave us liberty. Can the liberties of a nation be secure when we have removed a conviction that these liberties are the gift of God?" —Thomas Jefferson

<u>Laying a Wise Foundation</u>
The Founders may have asked aloud, "What do we want our government to be like?" But they actually had a deeper question in mind, which was, in essence, this: "What would God want our government to be like?"

There was no question as to the principles that should be set in place. The great debate was centered upon how to write those principles into a secularly-worded document that everyone could agree would be effective for allowing a republic to operate that would protect the people's liberty, while reining in the government with regard to its ability to infringe the selfsame rights the republic was instituted to safeguard. Just as God placed His law at the center of things, so the Founders placed the Constitution at the center, as well. Just as the People of Israel did not have government at its center—but God's Law—America would, likewise, not have government at its center, either—but, rather, the Constitution.

It is more than a little remarkable how closely the American Founders read and studied the Bible. When Harvard College was founded in 1636, the fact that the study of the Hebrew Bible would be a part of the curriculum, when instruction was to begin in 1638, was not in dispute. Since 1549, Hebrew had been required for an M.A. degree at the University of Cambridge, and the profile of Hebraic scholarship was heightened profoundly with the 1611 translation of the King James Bible.

Finding themselves in their own Land of Milk and Honey, and valuing religious freedom to the extent they did, perhaps it should come as no surprise that those who grew up in colonial America noticed some relevant parallels between themselves and the Israelites of biblical times. Modern-day America is all the better for its foundation having been firmly laid upon the time-tested wisdom of the Bible. And colonial Christians would have felt they were following in the footsteps of Jesus to foster the teachings of the Old Testament in their own lives. Indeed, in *Matthew 5:17*, Jesus says, "Do not imagine that I have come to set aside the Law or the Prophets. I have not come to abolish these things but to fulfill them."

"For the Lord is our judge, the Lord is our lawgiver, the Lord is our king; it is He who will save us." —Isaiah 33:22

<u>The Affirmation of the Three Parts of Governance</u>
God performs three functions in His governance of the People of Israel: Judge, Lawgiver, and King. These three roles are co-equal in the governing of a free society.

The judiciary is one branch of the government, and it must be able to function independently, as well as to provide a check on the power of the other two branches of government.

The legislature is, likewise, an independent function, as well as a check on the other branches of the government.

And the office of the American presidency has been created on the model of the unpretentious Israelite king, who was not above the law. This is why the President of the United States is not regal, but common, in how he is to be treated legally.

"When you are come unto the land which the Lord your God is giving you, and shall possess it, and shall dwell therein, and shall say, I will set a king over me, like as all the nations that are about me, you shall surely set a king, whom the Lord your God shall choose, one from among your countrymen you shall set as king over yourselves; you may not set a stranger over yourselves, which is not your countryman. Moreover, he shall not multiply horses for himself, nor shall he cause the people to return to Egypt to multiply horses, since the Lord has said to you, 'You shall never again return that way.' Neither shall he multiply wives to himself, that his heart turn not away; neither shall he greatly multiply to himself silver and gold. And it shall be, when he sits upon the throne of his kingdom, that he shall write himself a copy of this law in a book out of that which is before the Levite priests; and it shall be with him, and he shall read therein all the days of his life, that he may learn to fear the Lord his God, to keep all the words of this law and these statutes, to do them, that his heart be not lifted up above his countrymen, and that he turn not aside from the commandment, to the right hand, or to the left, to the end that he may prolong his days in his kingdom, he, and his children, in the midst of Israel."
—Deuteronomy 17:14-20

<u>On the Election & Duties of the Israelite King</u>
In ancient Israel, king is an office. The king must be born a citizen of the country he leads. This ensures that the king shares and values the culture of the people he will serve. This is why the President of the United States must be a natural-born citizen, in order to stand election. The US president is an "Israelite king," not an absolute monarch. He is even referred to as "president," "chief executive," or "commander-in-chief," in order to underscore this distinction.

High office, once attained, is for doing the people's business. The president's focus is to be on matters of state that are for the benefit of the people, not for his own benefit. He is the servant of the people; they are not his. He is there to safeguard their freedom, not to be enriched at their expense.

The chief executive is not above the law, nor does he enjoy any special legal privilege or protection. He must know the law intimately and abide by it and execute it faithfully, for he is not privileged in any way when it comes to legal matters. What is wrong for the people to do is also wrong for the executive. The Jewish king "shall write himself a copy of this law . . . and it shall be with him, and he shall read therein all the days of his life . . . to keep all the words of this law and these statutes, to do them, that his heart be not lifted up above his countrymen. . . ." The American president must also follow every single law to the letter, in order to lead by example. He must enforce the law, whether he be a lover of the law or not, for as long as it is the law of the land. Constitutionally-speaking, the president must "take care that the laws be faithfully executed."

The chief executive must maintain the state in the same condition in which he found it, upon taking office, so that all who come after him will have the same chances at health, wealth, and happiness with which he has been blessed. Thus, the president must govern according to the higher principles laid down by God in the Decalogue.

"The next day Moses sat as magistrate for the people, while the people stood around Moses from morning until evening. When Moses' father-in-law saw all that he was doing for the people, he said, 'What's this that you are doing for the people? Why do you sit alone, while all the people are standing around you from morning until evening?' Moses said to his father-in-law, 'Because the people come to me to inquire of God. When a conflict arises between them, they come to me and I judge between the two of them. I also teach them God's regulations and instructions.' Moses' father-in-law said to him, 'What you are doing isn't good. You will end up totally wearing yourself out, both you and these people who are with you. The work is too difficult for you. You can't do it alone. Now listen to me and let me give you some advice. And may God be with you! Your role should be to represent the people before God. You should bring their disputes before God yourself. Explain the regulations and instructions to them. Let them know the way they are supposed to go and the things they are supposed to do. But you should also look among all the people for capable persons who respect God. They should be trustworthy and not corrupt. Set these persons over the people as officers of groups of thousands, hundreds, fifties, and tens. Let them sit as judges for the people at all times. They should bring every major dispute to you, but they should decide all of the minor cases themselves. This will be much easier for you, and they will share your load. If you do this and God directs you, then you will be able to endure. And all these people will be able to go back to their homes much happier.'"* —Exodus 18:13-23

<u>The Wisdom of Jethro</u>
What Jethro teaches Moses is an approach to government where problems are solved at the lowest level possible. This mirrors the American system of township, county, state, and federal levels of problem-solving, where judicial appeals or legislative actions can go up the chain in the most important cases, for ultimate disposition.

This approach results in problem-solving with the greatest amount of freedom and flexibility possible. One-size-fits-all edicts from on high, that will saddle all of the people with the same prescription, are few and far between, in order to favor an approach that allows for more freedom closer to the problem at hand.

Such top-down policies should be principle-driven and universally applicable. They should be ethically-based and ought to describe the preferable approaches for adjudicating any and all disputes at every level of decision-making or problem-solving.

------

*"To inquire of God" = "To ask for justice (or God's judgment)" When an Israelite goes before Moses "to inquire of God," what he is actually doing, in this context, is going before God's law court to seek justice, with Moses sitting as judge and deciding matters in accord with God's law.

"When God finished speaking with Moses on Mount Sinai, he gave him the two tablets of the covenant, tablets of stone, written with the finger of God." —Exodus 31:18

<u>The Decalogue</u>
There are different ways of dividing into ten statements the sixteen verses of *Exodus 20:2-17*. The convention in use here is the oldest, according to ancient Jewish tradition, and this division probably would have been familiar to the Founders who undertook Hebrew studies at such places as Harvard College; but the true importance of these verses is in their establishment of the foundation for a free society. The interesting thing about the Decalogue (from the correct Greek translation of the Hebrew, meaning the Ten Words, or Ten Statements—not Ten Commandments) in terms of ancient history is that other societies outlawed crimes such as murder in phraseology tendentious of an "if . . . then" framework: "If a man knock out the tooth of his equal, his tooth shall be knocked out. . . . If he knock out the tooth of a freed man, he shall pay one-third of a gold mina." The Decalogue phrases such statements as absolutes, making them more than mere criminal infractions—but actually making them absolute wrongs. There is an idea present in Judaism—and by extension in Christianity—that God actually cares how human beings treat each other, regardless of gender, class, or place of origin.

The phrase "the Lord your God" is contained in each of the first five Statements of the Decalogue, because these are all about the relationship between the Lord God and His worship community. Even Statement Five, which instructs the People of Israel to honor parents, enables children to honor God, by first learning to honor earthly authority figures before being required to honor a heavenly Father.

The last five Statements are prohibitions regulating human behavior. There is no mention of God in any of them. But they are all phrased as being unconditionally wrong. The frame around the Ten Statements is this: the Decalogue begins with "I" (or, more comprehensively, "I am the Lord your God") and ends with "your neighbor."

"I am the Lord your God, Who brought you out of the land of Egypt, out of the house of bondage." —Exodus 20:2

<u>Statement One</u>
This verse, from *Exodus 20:2*, affirms that it is God who acts to provide freedom in human history. God is the source of all freedom, for obedience to His principles is what provides the conditions needed for freedom to exist. Moses is God's agent in the world whose actions bring the People of Israel out of slavery; thus he is a model for mankind. The Judeo-Christian God wants His children to be free.

So, personal freedom is necessary for a society to be moral, and vice-versa. If one is being compelled dictatorially to do a thing, he is not doing it out of goodness, because he has learned to love his fellows. He is doing it out of fear—fear of being punished.

The First Statement validates ethical monotheism, the faith that one God is the source of one ethical code of conduct that serves a higher purpose. In other words, human beings must all agree to serve an objective moral code that transcends human behavior based on selfish feelings. Also, there must be one standard for all humankind, whether they be government officials or common people. Just as the Jewish king must abide by the same morals and standards as the people, so must all government officials, across time and place. To have two differing moral codes would beg the question of which one is correct? And if a different standard of conduct is accepted for government officials, might they not then lead the people into immorality?

A people cannot be free, if it fall victim to its passions, or if it allow its leaders to do so; a people must behave ethically, according to the objective standards of Nature's God. Only self-control can bring freedom. And self-control stems from intentional effort, derived from one's conscience (as opposed to one's passions or feelings). To be moral, a people must divorce passion from decision-making; otherwise, it shall devolve into a culture where doing what passions dictate is regarded as worthy of doing, just because it feels right. This is why John Adams was concerned about virtue and morality, saying, "[I]t is religion and morality alone which can establish the principles upon which freedom can securely stand. The only foundation of a free constitution is pure virtue." John Adams also said, "[W]e have no government armed with power capable of contending with human passions unbridled by morality and religion. . . . Our constitution was made only for a moral and religious people. It is wholly inadequate to the government of any other."

Indeed, even people who do not profess a belief in God all benefit from living in a civil society where the majority does profess such a belief. And, even if nobody actually believed in God, the enactment of rules based on Judeo-Christian-style principles—as the objective set of standards by which to abide—would yet be necessary in order to make an ethical civil society possible.

"You shall have no other gods before Me. You shall not make for yourself a graven image, or any likeness of anything that is in heaven above, or that is in the earth beneath, or that is in the water under the earth. You shall not bow down to them or serve them, for I the Lord your God am a jealous God, visiting the iniquity of the fathers on the children to the third and the fourth generations of those who hate Me, but showing steadfast love to the thousandth generation of those who love Me and keep My commandments." —Exodus 20:3-6

<u>Statement Two</u>
The injunctions of this Statement, in *Exodus 20:3-6*, begins with the demand that the Israelites be faithful, as a wedding partner might be. The word *kanna*, meaning "impassioned" or "jealous," implies a bond similar to a marriage bond. God truly cares whether or not His children are faithful to Him. The statement that forbids a graven image is a reference to idol-making, not a prohibition against artistic creativity. The main issue of Statement Two is that of worshiping false gods. Anything that can lead one away from freedom and truth is a false god. The iniquity that is visited down through the generations on those who "hate" the Lord, by worshiping false gods, is a natural consequence of not following God's correct principles. The "steadfast love" that accrues to those who follow God's moral code is a natural outgrowth of correct living. A "law of attraction" is implied here: sow evil, reap evil; sow blessings, reap blessings.

The existence of only one Supreme Being means there is only one human race sharing the same deity, all people equal as brothers and sisters under one system of morality. Dennis Prager points out that passions such as love can be idols, if divorced from ethical values; his famous moral question is this: If your beloved dog and an unfamiliar stranger were drowning, who would you rescue? Many choose their dogs. "What we have here," contends Prager, "is the classic tension between feelings and values." Idolatry-based feelings can place a canine higher than a person.

If a cultural relativity is embraced that claims all life has equal worth, morality-based decision-making becomes subordinate to passion-driven decision-making, and this leads society away from ethically-based objectivity. The evil that develops from this mindset eventually requires comprehensive rule-making by the state, in order to protect people. The more immorality there is—due to a lack of enforcement of God's objective standards—the less freedom there can be.

Once America has lost the rule of law, and people begin to squabble over whose feelings are more valid and what is most "politically-correct" based upon a majority feeling (rather than upon an objective standard), liberty will be lost. The Founders believed that pure democracy was dangerous, since a majority could rob the minority of God-given, Natural Rights by a vote based upon the passions of the moment. This is why America was founded as a republic, with certain guarantees written into its framework that a simple majority cannot undo.

Cultural relativity is akin to allowing different gods to arise, each god ruling a separate passion. Every single human feeling is validated as the legitimate driver of some behavior and the outcomes that derive from it. This divergence from an objective moral code will mean much more fighting over whose passion-based values are correct, and, if judged on the basis of feelings, rather than against an objective standard, then everything becomes a matter of opinion. The only reason Hitler was wrong is because one feels he was wrong. So, what happens if one be disposed to feel differently? Does anti-Jewish, anti-Gypsy, anti-Slavic behavior now become acceptable, because it is driven by motives that "feel" valid to enough people? Diverging from a moral path will doom not only the current generation, but its children, and its children's children.

Another false idol that bears mentioning is addiction. Any addiction is based on human drives that are grounded in feelings. It is a good feeling that is being sought by the escape into drugs, overeating, promiscuity, or what-not. When one focuses on serving something that is higher than oneself, one must concentrate on using objective, ethical reasoning to decide on behavioral goals that ultimately work to move oneself away from being ruled by base feelings and urges.

Holding to an objective, higher morality, backed by the rule of law, will bless many generations yet to come, as long as a society holds true to God's higher values as shared by Moses the Lawgiver.

"You shall not carry the name of the Lord your God in vain, for the Lord will not hold him guiltless who carries his name in vain." —Exodus 20:7

<u>Statement Three</u>
In Hebrew, *nasa* means "to carry," not "to take." Carrying the Lord's name in vain, per *Exodus 20:7*, is committing evil in God's name—the one unforgivable sin. Saying, "Oh, God!" is not unpardonable; but murdering in God's name is. Suicide bombers, Islamic terrorists, and jihadist mass-murderers are the most obvious examples of sinners who carry God's name in vain, but God also condemns Jews, Christians, or any others who commit crimes in His name.

Evil done in God's name damages His reputation. And without belief in divine morality, the reining in of passion becomes rare, freedom untenable. Anyone who commits an evil deed, and uses God as a justification, is committing an unpardonable act. This is because that person is not just sinning, but also teaching others that commission of the particular sin in question is at God's behest, or with God's permission. Even if this teaching is only by example—such as a jihadist shouting out "Allahu akbar!" as he blows himself up, killing "infidels" in the process—it serves as a powerful false lesson to many. This act teaches that perpetrating evil is an acceptable thing in the eyes of God; it also causes many others to believe that all religious people are immoral or crazy, regardless of the kind of religious upbringing they may have experienced; thus, many people may well conclude that all religious people are murderous or, at a minimum, unhealthy to be around.

This prohibition against carrying God's name in vain also applies to perjury in a law court, when a religious oath is taken to tell the truth. Even if the lie goes undetected by the court, God will ultimately hold the liar accountable. The more immediate result may well be that the oath breaker, having gotten away with committing an injustice, will feel encouraged to repeat such behavior until, ultimately, his lying is detected by authorities and punished by the court.

"Remember the Sabbath day, to keep it holy. Six days you shall labor, and do all your work, but the seventh day is a Sabbath to the Lord your God. On it you shall not do any work, you, or your son, or your daughter, your male servant, or your female servant, or your livestock, or the foreigner who is within your gates. For in six days the Lord made heaven and earth, the sea, and all that is in them, and rested on the seventh day. Therefore the Lord blessed the Sabbath day and made it holy." —Exodus 20:8-11

<u>Statement Four</u>
According to *Exodus 20:8-11*, human beings are created in God's image, and, as God took the seventh day off, human beings are to do likewise, making the seventh day always a holy day (or a holiday). Nowhere in the ancient world, except among the Hebrews, did there exist a seven-day division of time. Other cultures observed lunar and solar cycles only, which set the Hebrew God apart from all others, existing outside of, or beyond, nature and its rhythms.

No one is to work on the Sabbath, not even animals. Every creature of God is to exercise some freedom, for those who labor non-stop are in bondage to work and, therefore, unfree. And God does not desire slaves, nor does He want the bad outcomes that go with not being free. Some amount of time set aside, regularly, for study and reflection is desirable, in order that human beings may enable themselves to create and renew, on an ongoing basis, a moral and happy society.

This divinely-ordained freedom from work enhances relationships, thus strengthening the culture of civil society. If one works all the time, one never gets to exercise or strengthen one's personal ethics as a free moral agent. The workplace is full of dictates and guidelines. People do as they are told, and there is little room for ethical thought or evaluation on a personal level. And, in some professions, such as law, the ethics are quite divorced from life in a free civil society. Commitment to a periodic holiday away from work—wherein one must study, exercise, and teach love and morality—is the purpose of taking a sabbatical at least one day a week.

"Honor your father and your mother, that your days may be long in the land that the Lord your God is giving you." —Exodus 20:12

<u>Statement Five</u>
If people respect parents and authority figures, as *Exodus 20:12* commands, freedom will continue in perpetuity. *Leviticus 19:3*, it should be noted, is a reiteration of the Ten Statements that reverses the parental order, listing the mother first; this is to teach children that both parents must be respected equally. Love is not required, but honoring authority is. Children who honor parents also learn to respect other authority figures, as well as the authority of God and God's Law. People who learn to do this fall less frequently into trouble.

If parents are abusive of their children to the point of alienating them altogether, those children still need to learn to honor parental authority figures—or guardians. Without learning to respect authority, a child risks developing unhealthy, freedom-compromising relationships. The child will seek out people that feel good to be around and will learn only to respect—or follow directives from—people who inspire good feelings. This will mean, in the future, bad people who seem nice will command bad behavior and get it. Also, good people who are officious or uncomfortable people to be around may command good behavior and not get it. This explains why *honoring* parental authority figures must be the key value, and not necessarily *loving* them.

"You shall not murder." —Exodus 20:13

<u>Statement Six</u>
The immoral or unlawful taking of a human life—murder—is what is at issue in *Exodus 20:13*. (In King James' day, "kill" was used synonymously with "murder"—which is why "Thou shalt not kill" was chosen as an appropriate translation of the Hebrew, although this is no longer the case.) Taking a life in an act of war, or for purposes of capital punishment, is not immoral. God does not condemn the death penalty, nor does He condone pacifism.

The death penalty for someone who has stolen bread would certainly be worthy of God's condemnation, since this would not be a fair penalty, where the punishment fits the crime. It must, by the same token, be noted that invoking pacifism, in the face of Nazi genocide or some equally-great evil, may also prove to be wrong-headed to the point of being sinful in many instances.

Murder is a category of sin for which one cannot repent, since the person whose pardon must be solicited is no longer alive to give such a pardon. Murder is the ultimate theft of freedom.

"You shall not commit adultery." —Exodus 20:14

<u>Statement Seven</u>
Adultery, in the Seventh Statement of *Exodus 20:14*, is meant as sexual intercourse that has been consented to by both lovers, at least one of whom is married or betrothed. This crime is treated as both a civil wrong and a sin against God, which is why the spouse who has been offended has no power to pardon either party to the offense.

This inability of the person wronged to do any pardoning is why this sin is ranked between the sins of murder and stealing. The bond violated is one that is of a sacred nature.

Civil society depends, to an extent, on stability, and the stability of families is an important component of civil society. Having sex outside of marriage threatens both family civility and family stability in a way that can affect the overall society in terms of creating both incivility and instability within the society at large. The injured parties carry ill feelings with them into their daily interactions with others, and the perpetrators of the adulterous relationships set bad examples for others who see what they have done. The entire community suffers.

Spousal monogamy enforces emotional maturity and family commitment. This protects children from growing up in an environment that is devoid of the needed civility or stability for them to mature properly. Therefore, the injury caused by the adulterer is not to the spouse alone, which means that the spouse is not at liberty to forgive the adultery. Nor do other family members fully understand the nature of the offense against them, and, due to this fact, the children and extended family also have no standing to forgive the adulterer, just as community members may not do so.

Children do best when they see parents who make love an action verb that they are committed to enacting on a daily basis, rather than a false god—a feeling—that they serve as slaves (therefore the adultery). When objectively-based decisions are being made for the family because they are right, regardless of what the parents feel like doing, this promotes healthy and mature family stability. Children reared in this kind of environment will learn to trust people more and will, as a result, seek out people's advice and teaching. The prohibition of adultery also protects children from incest, since all incestuous affairs are adulterous relationships.

Adulterous affairs promote dishonesty. Adultery is never allowed, even if both partners agree to an open relationship, for it poses a threat to the family, setting a bad example for those watching. Morally responsible parental modeling is needed to maintain a free society, with stability and predictability, based upon trust and rule of law. Uncommitted parents with no accountability to spouses fail to create stability and trust, producing scofflaws who become flouters of the rule of law. Only responsible citizens can be trusted with freedom; responsibility and freedom coincide.

"You shall not steal." —Exodus 20:15

<u>Statement Eight</u>
The prohibition against theft, from *Exodus 20:15*, encompasses most of the sin in the world. A biblical expert will point out that murder is stealing a life; adultery, stealing a spouse; perjury, stealing justice. Other things which can be stolen are these: a person's reputation, through gossip; a person's dignity, through humiliation; a person's intellectual property, through plagiarism; a person's freedom, by kidnaping; a person's trust, by lying; or private property, by thievery.

Slavery among the Israelites in the Bible is what would generally be referred to as "debt slavery," or "indentured servitude," not slavery by kidnaping, which is absolutely prohibited by the Eighth Statement.

Private property rights are a necessary condition for there to be freedom. Stealing property destroys freedom. State appropriation, or control, of property means state dictation of property rules—thus no freedom of action. This is outright thievery, a miscarriage of justice by any measure.

John Adams knew that, once the government started to use its power to appropriate property from some to give to others, America would begin down the road to decline, for this kind of redistribution would violate the Principle of Agency (that the government, as the public's agent, may not do anything, unless it also be moral for a citizen to do the same; taking money or property from one person for redistribution to another, without the owner's permission, is immoral and illegal for an individual to do, so the government may not do it). Quoth Adams, "The moment the idea is admitted into society that property is not as sacred as the laws of God, and that there is not a force of law and public justice to protect it, anarchy and tyranny commence. If 'Thou shalt not covet,' and 'Thou shalt not steal,' were not commandments of Heaven, they must be made inviolable precepts in every society, before it can be civilized or made free."

Adams knew that people who work hard to succeed find themselves able to employ others as a result or, by saving money, empower the bank to use the money towards the same ends, by investing in corporations and extending loans to businesses. These high earners would stop trying so hard to benefit themselves or others, if their property, their wealth, were confiscated for redistribution among those who do little—or nothing at all. Such wealth redistribution would kill the proverbial goose that lays the golden eggs, and the production of wealth would slow to a crawl, harming business owner and working person alike, by impoverishing them all as an unhappy outcome of a misguided policy that allows theft from some to buy the votes of others.

"You shall not give false witness against your neighbor." —Exodus 20:16

<u>Statement Nine</u>
Exodus 20:16 teaches that a free society cannot operate, if it be based upon any system that tolerates or engenders falsehood. There must be justice, based upon rule of law, in order to maintain freedom. People must be able to act, free of false accusations. Predictability and stability are needed, in order to plan one's personal life or one's business affairs.

Also, such issues as Holocaust-denial—as well as other forms of lying—divide people on issues that would not exist, if truth were the basis for all information. Dishonest journalism that lies by misrepresentation, or by omission, harms civil society and the dual causes of freedom and morality as well.

Lying for a "good cause" is immoral, because misrepresenting a problem can cause a misallocation of limited resources to cure it. If too many resources were allocated to one problem, a second problem might go needlessly unsolved. In the end, people are hurt. A good example of this might be a person who exaggerates the number of times he has been threatened by hooligans, in order to get the police to step up their patrols in his neighborhood. If the solution entail too many patrols—a focus beyond what is actually necessary—as a result of the person's exaggeration, other areas that are more in need of policing may go without sorely-needed police protection. The outcome of this misallocation of resources could even entail an unfortunate injury or a death that might have been prevented.

"You shall not covet your neighbor's house; you shall not covet your neighbor's wife, or his male servant, or his female servant, or his ox, or his donkey, or anything that is your neighbor's." —Exodus 20:17

<u>Statement Ten</u>
Exodus 20:17 is the only one of the Ten Statements that prohibits a thought. The reason is because of the incredible destruction that is wrought by coveting! The Hebrew word *lakhmohd* means desiring something owned by another to the point of planning to steal it. This thought process of coveting produces most of the sinning in the world. Avoidance of coveting, on the other hand, begets the moral responsibility that supports a free society.

"America will never be destroyed from the outside. If we falter and lose our freedoms, it will be because we destroyed ourselves." —Abraham Lincoln

<u>Ethics, Responsibility, & Freedom</u>
Ethically enforced rule of law and responsible self-control must work together to enable a society based on freedom. The Decalogue lays the necessary foundation, across time and space, to all who would heed its precepts. But it is the responsibility of all who strive to be free to continue to teach the ethical principles that are needed for liberty to endure. The duty to do this is inscribed onto the Liberty Bell itself: "Proclaim LIBERTY throughout all the Land unto all the Inhabitants thereof LEV XXV X." It is not a onetime event that is being called for, but an ongoing obligation.

James Madison wrote in Federalist No. 49 that, contrary to the passions of the moment, "it is the reason, alone, of the public, that ought to control and regulate the government. The passions ought to be controlled and regulated by the government." A strong system of checks and balances, today often disparagingly referred to as "gridlock," is desperately needed in a republic, in order to ensure that new laws are made only after a good deal of reflection and debate, and with the broadest consensus possible.

In moments of passion, the best, most moral, decisions are not generally made. It is thoughtful reflection, based upon Judeo-Christian principles, that best guarantees that a higher purpose will be served, for the good of all concerned, when new policies are instituted among the people.

Stephen Covey once said that "you cannot break a principle; you can only break yourself against it." Decisions made in the heat of passion, based upon wishful thinking about how things might turn out, run the risk of generating results that could be catastrophic for the large majority of citizens. In some cases, such decisions could even end up compromising individual freedom and the moral choices available to the people.

Ronald Reagan, America's 40th president, once made the following statement: "Freedom is never more than one generation away from extinction. We didn't pass it to our children in the bloodstream. It must be fought for, protected, and handed on for them to do the same, or one day we will spend our sunset years telling our children and our children's children what it was once like in the United States where men were free."

All Americans—by the examples of their lives and by their teachings to others—must take it upon themselves to empower friends, family members, and future generations to live morally and responsibly. Americans must teach and reteach, on an ongoing basis, the value of freedom to each other, by promoting ethically-based enlightenment and principled reflection. Americans must always remain mindful that only a morality-based civil society and a Constitutionally-limited government can secure the blessings of liberty—for all people, for all time.

Appendix K: Evaluating Thomas Jefferson & America's Founding Documents

"If we are made in some degree for others, yet in a greater are we made for ourselves. It were contrary to feeling and indeed ridiculous to suppose that a man had less rights in himself than one of his neighbors, or indeed all of them put together. This would be slavery, and not that liberty which the bill of rights has made inviolable, and for the preservation of which our government has been charged." —Thomas Jefferson

"Now, take the Constitution according to its plain reading, and I defy the presentation of a single pro-slavery clause in it. On the other hand it will be found to contain principles and purposes entirely hostile to the existence of slavery." —Frederick Douglass

Evaluating Jefferson

Thomas Jefferson stands accused by many of being immoral, and his seminal role in America's founding is often voiced as a valid reason for condemning America's founding as racist from birth. But this accusation is simplistic, lacking nuance or serious consideration of the historical context within which Thomas Jefferson lived. It also ignores many important facts of Jefferson's biography, many of which are quite striking. While such an unsophisticated estimation may be excusable for neophytes, seasoned scholars and caring teachers have little to excuse them for such intellectual simplicity and counterfactual instruction. Or dare I say dishonesty? Absent from most erroneous evaluations of Jefferson is an honest accounting of Jefferson's own personal actions to seek the abolition of slavery.

Teresa Sullivan, President of the University of Virginia, (according to an article entitled "Professors ask Sullivan to stop quoting Jefferson," published on November 11, 2016, in *The Cavalier Daily*) has written of Jefferson's claim that "all men are created equal" that "[t]hose words were inherently contradictory in an era of slavery, but because of their power, they became the fundamental expression of a more genuine equality today." Dr. Sullivan wrote those words in response to an accusation that it was inappropriate for her to quote the University of Virginia's founder, due to the fact that Jefferson was a slaveholder. While it is true that Jefferson owned slaves, the amount of good that he accomplished in his life—as well as the ongoing use of his words to promote equal rights—merits thoughtful reflection before ultimately deciding to condemn Thomas Jefferson altogether.

Jefferson was, in fact, an energetic opponent of slavery, believing it to be contrary to Natural Law. Jefferson referred to slavery as a "moral depravity" and a "hideous blot." As the Revolutionary War was raging, Jefferson was actively working to abolish the slave trade. Although Jefferson would succeed, by his leadership efforts, in 1778, in banning the importation of slaves into his home state, making Virginia one of the first jurisdictions worldwide to ban the practice, he would not succeed, as Virginia's governor, in banning slavery altogether, although he would make the attempt.

<u>Jefferson's Denunciation of Slavery in His Original Draft of the Declaration</u>
Despite the fact that Jefferson inherited slaves from his father and acquired slaves by marriage, *he would fight his entire adult life to abolish the South's Peculiar Institution, famously denouncing slavery in his original draft of the Declaration of Independence*, complaining about King George III's unprincipled promotion of human trafficking: **"He has waged cruel war against human nature itself, violating its most sacred rights of life and liberty in the persons of a distant people who never offended him, captivating & carrying them into slavery in another hemisphere or to incur miserable death in their transportation thither. This piratical warfare, the opprobrium of infidel powers, is the warfare of the Christian King of Great Britain. Determined to keep open a market where Men should be bought & sold, he has prostituted his negative for suppressing every legislative attempt to prohibit or restrain this execrable commerce. And that this assemblage of horrors might want no fact of distinguished die*, he is now exciting those very people to rise in arms among us, and to purchase that liberty of which he has deprived them, by murdering the people on whom he has obtruded them: thus paying off former crimes committed against the Liberties of one people, with crimes which he urges them to commit against the lives of another."** After the Revolutionary War was over, in 1784, Jefferson proposed a ban on slavery in the Northwest Territory. Jefferson also devised a plan to improve the treatment of slaves and then to emancipate slaves by degrees, making every child born after a certain date a free person.

Jefferson wrote that hanging onto slavery was like holding "a wolf by the ear, and we can neither hold him, nor safely let him go." Jefferson thought that America, the world's first true democratic republic, might eventually be destroyed by slavery, if the institution were not ended. And Jefferson turned out to be right. The Union was indeed brought to an end over slavery, dying a bloody death in a terrible civil war. It was Abraham Lincoln who would eventually restore the Union as a country with freedom for all, according to the nation's original promissory note.

During Jefferson's time as President of the United States, it was he who, in 1807, would sign a law criminalizing the importation of slaves into the United States, in line with the 1808 Clause of the US Constitution, an action which, in concert with England's decision to do likewise, would effectively abolish the legitimate international slave trade. While Jefferson lived an imperfect, often conflicted, human life, his more judgmental critics tend to convict him in their minds as a villain through and through, typically with very little to offer in the way of complex analysis—let alone an appreciation—of this Founding Father's righteous accomplishments. Any attempt at a nuanced approach to Jefferson is generally seen by Jefferson's most severe detractors as racist on the face of it, a view which tends to oversimplify the issue unfairly.

<u>Frederick Douglass Believed in America's Founding</u>
The truth about Thomas Jefferson is that he—along with other Founding Fathers—was, and is, an important influence upon the way Americans conceptualize freedom to this day. Frederick Douglass, a famous American abolitionist and lecturer who escaped from slavery, valued Jefferson's words as written in the Declaration of Independence, as well as believing in the

language of freedom contained within the US Constitution. Douglass did not believe that America's founding documents were racist but saw, instead, a blueprint for freedom that all men—being "created equal"—had the right to enjoy. Douglass comprehended the Constitution in all its subtlety, seeing it as the blessing that it is and understanding the intentions of the 3/5 Clause as a reward for any slave states that might free their slaves (since freemen would count as an entire person in the census, thereby increasing a state's representation in the Congress as a consequence of freeing slaves).

What Frederick Douglass understood about full-blown Americanism was this: While the Declaration illuminates the philosophy of American liberty, by using 27 complaints against injustice to shed light upon crucial issues, it is the Constitution that eventually provides permanent solutions to those issues, by establishing a free republic that protects the rights of every individual equally. The plain language of the Constitution, to borrow the words of George Washington, "gives to bigotry no sanction, to persecution no assistance." And Douglass knew it.

<u>America's Ever-Unfolding Promissory Note</u>
Whatever their shortcomings, America's Founders understood they were not perfect. They knew, however, that even an imperfect birth of freedom would provide America with the opportunity for a great and, hopefully, unending experiment. The blueprint for this experiment in individual liberty, that they wrote into the US Constitution, would provide its inheritors with an ever-unfolding promissory note for the sustenance and enlargement of life, liberty, and the pursuit of happiness throughout the ages. It was a freedom big enough to encompass any and all races, creeds, and colors, so long as they would only make common cause with lovers of liberty.

The Constitution America's Founders bestowed upon their country is written in a neutral style, without specific references to race or gender. President Reagan referred to America's constitutional republic as a "shining city on a hill" and the "last best hope for man on earth." If those words are to remain true, American patriots must jealously protect the promissory note embedded in the US Constitution for every American generation yet to come. Thomas Jefferson would have wished it, Frederick Douglass would have approved, and modern-day patriots should all strive to pass on America's rich heritage and the lessons learned from the country's history that blesses every free American.

---

distinguished die [honorable dye] = venerable color
"And that this assemblage of horrors might want no fact of distinguished die*, he is now exciting those very people to rise in arms among us, and to purchase that liberty of which he has deprived them."
["And that this assemblage of horrors might lack no fact of honorable (skin) color*, he is now exciting those very people to rise in arms among us, and to purchase that liberty of which he has deprived them.]